Savory Pies

Delicious Recipes for Seasoned Meats, Vegetables
and Cheeses Baked in Perfectly Flaky Crusts

Savory Pies

Delicious Recipes for Seasoned Meats, Vegetables and Cheeses Baked in Perfectly Flaky Crusts

GREG HENRY

with wine notes by
Grant Henry

Ulysses Press

Published by
Ulysses Press
P.O. Box 3440
Berkeley, CA 94703
www.ulyssespress.com

A Hollan Publishing, Inc. Concept

ISBN: 978-1-61243-106-2
Library of Congress Catalog Number 2012940434

Printed in the United States by Bang Printing

10 9 8 7 6 5 4 3 2 1

Acquisitions Editor: Keith Riegert
Managing Editor: Claire Chun
Editor: Phyllis Elving
Proofreader: Lauren Harrison
Design and layout: what!design @ whatweb.com
Cover photographs: © Greg Henry *front:* arugula, black olive, and sun-dried tomato calzone; jerk-spiced meat patties; roasted radish tart; sweet sausage cabbage pie *back:* Irish breakfast pie; mushroom, goat cheese, and mint hand pies; shaved asparagus galette; BBQ chicken empanadas; baked egg shakshuka; pot roast hand pies with cheddar

To Ken, who listened to me read recipes aloud at night as if each were a mini version of the greatest story ever told. Twenty-plus years and still the pie of my eye.

TABLE OF CONTENTS

Main Course Pies—Vegetarian

Hand Pies 15 Recipes

ACKNOWLEDGMENTS

It takes a village—a pie-eating, pie-making, pie-loving village. Fortunately, the blogosphere is just such a village. So many talented people came to the rescue all throughout this pie-maker's journey.

Many of the props you see in this book are way too swanky to be mine. Friends and extended family all contributed key pieces. Their good taste was so important in giving this book some of its visual appeal. Most particularly, I would like to thank Jackie Dodd/*The Beeroness*; Erika Penzer Kerekes/*In Erika's Kitchen*; Miyoshi Barosh; Laura Pangrazio; Rocco Vienhage; and my neighbors Laura Smith and Michael Doret, who showed up at the door—vintage fork in hand—whenever I rang.

I can't forget the cooks in my life, called upon to test recipes at various stages in this process. They neither pulled punches nor sugarcoated a single savory pie. I'm grateful to Tori Avey/*The Shiksa in the Kitchen*; Kris Bingham; Jane Bonacci/*The Heritage Cook*; Kim Burnell/*Rustic Garden Bistro*; Steven Dunn/*Oui, Chef*; Allison Guinn; Jenny Johnson/*Vintage Sugarcube*; Renee Joslyn/*Flamingo Musings*; Trevor Kensey/*sis.boom.[blog!]*; Liz Lees; Suzanne Morrell; Dorothy Reinhold/*Shockingly Delicious*; Elizabeth Schmitt/*Liz the Chef*; Janis Tester/*Bite Me New England*; Amy Torres; and Svetlana Watkins/*Bibberche*.

Of course, I can't forget the Big Cheese. Everything I know about cheese I learned because of Barrie Lynn, the Cheese Impresario. We'll always have Wisconsin.

Finally, special thanks to Nathan Hazard and Andy Windak, who ate pie and listened to me talk late into the night—even after listening to my blather all through a recording session of "The Table Set."

INTRODUCTION

Savory pies are like a well-loved blanket: warm, satisfying, and marvelously easy to snuggle into. That may explain why most cuisines around the world include some kind of savory pie. Tarts, galettes, cobblers, and even cute little hand pies are among the 62 creative and comforting savory pies that make an appearance in this book. What binds them all together is the fact that not one of these warm-from-the-oven beauties is for dessert.

Why should you wait until dessert to eat pie? Pies can be combinations of just about anything you imagine. Cheese, meat, vegetables, even seafood—they're even better when wrapped, tucked, or baked inside a delectable crust. Sometimes flaky, sometimes chewy. Crunchy. Crisp. Buttery.

Cooks love savory pies because the combination of a tender, salted crust and a hearty filling is elementally simple yet endlessly variable. There's a savory pie to fit every mood and appetite, from the Irish pub–inspired goodness of beef and Guinness to piping-hot American pot pies to rustic, fist-sized pasties. Savory Pies takes an international approach, including fragrant jerk-spiced pockets from the Caribbean, innovative empanadas from Argentina, and French *tartes* made modern. Italy's molten calzone makes a pared-down appearance as a vegetarian delight. Nearly every possible combination of beloved ingredients is presented in a perfect little package designed to be savored.

A pie can be a quick family meal or an elegant prelude to a formal dinner. Hand pies make an easy lunch on the run and are a staple in cultures where street food rules. Pies are perfect for the holidays, of course, but how about brunch? Pies make great gifts, they travel well, and they are welcome additions to potluck parties. They're perfect for a housewarming or as a thoughtful offering to a new neighbor. Best of all, pies always look spectacular. Because the pastry acts as a wrapping, it automatically elevates even the simplest ingredients. Rustic or elegant, pies have a visual appeal that draws people to the table.

—Greg Henry

A WORD ABOUT WINE

The wine selections that accompany many of these recipes were made with an eye toward easy-to-find wines, staying away from wines that would require selling a major organ to purchase them. The focus is more on the style of the wine than on particular grape varietals or producers, because there are so many great wines beyond the obvious choices. Most importantly, if these selections aren't available, find a good wine shop, tell the staff what's on the menu, and don't be afraid to let them take you on a journey.

—Grant Henry

Three Tips for the Pie Maker

Store-Bought Crusts. If making pastry scares you and will keep you from trying your hand at pie, by all means use store-bought crusts. But let me warn you, I've tried them all and they're not all the same.

For me, the "just add water" dry mixes are the least successful—partly because they're no less work than making pastry from scratch.

The frozen "ready to fill" variety is about as easy as it gets, though you're limited to an open, single-crust pie. But that flimsy foil "pie plate" really ruins it for me. It just doesn't say lovin' from the oven.

The rolled crust found in the refrigerated section of the grocery store isn't bad, though penny for penny, pie for pie, it's a rather expensive convenience. It's also a bit bland for my taste, though it bakes up with impressive flakiness and allows flexibility in both size and construction. Be aware that sometimes the flakiness and ease of handling come from hydrogenated fat, so check the box and your comfort level before you buy.

Finally—puff pastry. A good all-butter purchased puff pastry is better than what I can make myself, especially the French brands. I depend on these when making pies that call for puff pastry. They can be kept in the freezer until you're ready to use them—but please thaw the frozen crust slowly, in the refrigerator. The scraps save well, provided you handle them well. Don't wad them in a ball. Take the time to stack the shards and roll them out into a flat piece about ¼ inch thick, then fold into a convenient size for storage. This is the best way to assure that those million flaky layers will puff up to golden perfection.

Blind Baking. Sometimes a recipe asks you to prebake the pastry, as in the Roasted Radish Tart with Arugula and Bagna Cauda (page 43). Technically this is called "blind baking"—not a very helpful term, is it? "Prebaking" is a lot more intuitive. Or is it? A novice might read that term, roll out the dough, line a pie pan, and pop it in the oven. If you've ever done that (and who hasn't?), you know that you'll probably end up with a misshapen, shrunken crust that's puffed up in all the wrong places. So let me lead you from the darkness of "blind baking" into the light of "prebaking."

Start with well-chilled dough. Roll it out carefully (see opposite). Once the dough has been eased into the pan, use the tines of a fork to pierce holes along the bottom to let steam escape. Then cut a piece of foil or parchment paper big enough to hang over the edge by a couple of inches all around. (You can use cupcake liners on small individual tarts.) Fill the foil- or parchment-lined pie shell with weights. You can buy pie weights for just such a purpose, but beans or rice are acceptable, too; they need to be discarded afterward or set aside for this purpose only. *The Pie and Pastry Bible* author Rose Levy Beranbaum recommends copper pennies, which are terrific heat conductors. If you are particularly fussy (like me), you can tie up your weights in a pouch of double-thick cheesecloth, making them a cinch to remove.

Rolling the Dough. I always fear that recipes make pie dough way too complicated. But this is a cookbook. You expect recipes, right? So I've included some crust recipes. But once you've made a few pies you'll learn to recognize what makes the dough work—because your climate, your kitchen, even your hands play a role in making great pie dough.

Once you've made great pie dough, knowing how to roll it out becomes important. Take your time and think like the dough thinks. Glutens are predictable but sometimes stubborn, and they have a memory, so let them rest and relax in the refrigerator for at least an hour.

When you're ready to roll, give yourself some room. Make sure the dough is well-chilled, but don't be afraid to let it sit for a few moments. Punch your thumb into it. The glutens will tell you when the temperature is right. The indentation should set easily to thumb pressure; very soft dough needs more chilling. Chilling is important. It's when the moisture gets properly distributed.

When the dough says so, lightly dust your work surface with flour; keep extra flour nearby—just in case. The rolling pin and in some cases your hands will need flour, too, because you'll use these to flatten your disc or square of dough before you start. Flip, pat, and dust the dough and the work surface a few more times before you get going.

Now here comes the key. Don't press the dough or force it in any particular fashion. Let the dough guide your rolling pin. Start in the center and roll out toward the edge. Flip and flop the dough as you work, turning it over and making quarter turns as you go. Use more flour, both on the dough and on the work surface, if the dough tells you to. The rolling pin may need some as well. Rolling pie dough is as Zen as it gets. So get into the moment and enjoy the process.

You'll notice that my pie dough recipes are generous in proportion. That's because I want you to enjoy rolling the dough. I don't want you to worry if you're doing it just right. My recipes should give you plenty of leeway to roll your rounds at least a couple of inches bigger than you need. This makes for neat, clean edges. Neat, clean edges make you feel like you know what you're doing. Feeling confident in your abilities is the very first step in making great pie.

THE CRUSTS

Basic Pie Pastry

Crisp, flaky, and just salty enough. Creating a crust with "tooth" that melts instantly on your tongue is the key to any great pie. But opinions and controversies abound. What combination or ratio is best? Well, I've tried them all. The all-butter crust remains my favorite for its rich, savory flavor. Its four simple ingredients are always on hand at my house, so in my opinion, this is the one to master.

MAKES TWO 8 TO 10-INCH PIE CRUSTS OR ONE 8 TO 10-INCH DOUBLE-CRUST SHELL

2¾ cups (390 grams) all-purpose flour, scooped and leveled, plus more as needed

1 teaspoon kosher salt

2 sticks (1 cup) plus 2 tablespoons very cold European-style (high-fat) unsalted butter, cut into ½-inch dice

2 or 3 ice cubes

⅓ cup cold water (plus 2 tablespoons, if needed)

In the bowl of a food processor, pulse the 2¾ cups flour with the salt 5 or 6 times until well combined. If a specific recipe calls for additional spices, herbs, cheese, vinegar, or lemon juice, this is the time to add them.

Add the butter and pulse 10 or 12 more times until the mixture is crumbly and coarse, with various-size chunks of butter visible throughout. Wedge 2 or 3 ice cubes, broken up if necessary, in the processor's feed tube. With the machine running, pour up to ⅓ cup cold water over the ice in the ice-filled feed tube a tablespoon at a time, until the dough just comes together and begins to pull cleanly away from the sides of the bowl in jagged clumps. Don't let the machine run too long, and don't worry if you don't use all the water. Overworked dough and/or too much water are the main culprits in making pastry tough or dense. However, in warm weather or dry climates you may need up to 2 tablespoons more cold water. You'll learn to recognize the right balance of wet and dry.

Move the dough to a lightly floured work surface and gently knead it 2 or 3 times. If it seems quite sticky or at all wet, sprinkle in another few teaspoons flour. Give it a couple more quick, gentle kneads. Divide the dough in half and shape into 2 discs about 5 inches in diameter and ¾ inch thick, or as indicated in the individual recipe. Wrap in plastic and refrigerate at least 1 hour (or up to 2 days) to distribute the moisture evenly, or freeze for up to 1 month.

Cream Cheese Crust

I promise you there's no great secret to making good pastry dough. Once you've done it a few times you'll recognize the right balance of wet to dry and the elasticity that makes dough easy to work without being too dense. But no matter how many times I make that promise, I still see fear in the eyes of the novice baker. I usually try to talk them down from the pie precipice with this recipe, because it's so forgiving. It's easy as pie! (I couldn't write this whole book and let that lowball pass by.)

MAKES TWO 8 TO 10-INCH PIE CRUSTS OR ONE 8 TO 10-INCH DOUBLE-CRUST SHELL

6 ounces cream cheese, at room temperature

1 stick (½ cup) plus 2 tablespoons European-style (high-fat) unsalted butter, at room temperature

2 tablespoons heavy cream, or more as needed

2¾ cups (390 grams) all-purpose flour, scooped and leveled, plus more as needed

1 teaspoon kosher salt

Place the cream cheese, butter, and cream in the bowl of a food processor and process until well combined and fluffy, about 20 seconds. Add the 2¾ cups flour and the salt; pulse 5 or 6 times. Scrape the sides with a rubber spatula and process another 15 to 20 seconds, until the dough just comes together and begins to pull cleanly away from the sides in jagged clumps. If this doesn't happen, add another few teaspoons of cream, as needed.

Move the dough to a lightly floured work surface and gently knead 2 or 3 times. If it seems quite sticky or at all wet, sprinkle on another few teaspoons flour and give it a couple more quick, gentle kneads. Divide the dough in half and shape into 2 discs about 5 inches in diameter and ¾ inch thick, or as indicated in the individual recipe. Wrap in plastic and refrigerate at least 1 hour (or up to 2 days), or freeze for up to 1 month.

NOTE

High-fat, European-style butter is essential for a perfect pie crust. Along with the chilling, it's what makes the dough flaky and minimizes shrinking. Many people swear that adding 1 tablespoon white vinegar or lemon juice guarantees a flaky crust. I'm on the fence, but you can add these if you want, adjusting the water accordingly.

Easy Flatbread Dough

Let's face it—even with a great dough recipe, pizza is hard for the home cook to perfect. Most of our kitchens just aren't equipped with an oven that gets hot enough to do the job well, so I haven't included a single standard-size, brick oven–style pizza pie recipe in this book. Smaller flatbread versions such as pizzettes or calzoni are much easier to handle at home. I promise that with a good pizza stone and a 500°F oven, you'll be pleased with these little pies and their chewy, slightly charred crusts.

MAKES 1½ POUNDS (SEE SPECIFIC RECIPES FOR THEIR YIELDS)

2 teaspoons (¼ ounce) active dry yeast

Big pinch of sugar

1 cup warm (about 110°F) milk or water, plus more water if needed (see note)

3 cups (375 grams) all-purpose flour, plus more as needed, divided

1 teaspoon kosher salt

¼ cup extra-virgin olive oil, plus more for greasing bowl

2 teaspoons honey

In the bowl of a stand mixer, dissolve the yeast and sugar in the warm milk or water. Set aside until frothy, about 10 minutes.

Add 2½ cups flour, salt, ¼ cup olive oil, and honey to the mixer bowl. Run the mixer on low, using the dough hook; after a minute or so, slowly sprinkle in another ½ cup flour. Watch the dough and dribble in small amounts of water if needed to keep it elastic. The dough should begin to look very smooth, pulling cleanly away from the sides and bottom of the bowl, after about 10 minutes. If this doesn't happen, add a few more tablespoons flour and continue running the mixer until it does.

Transfer the dough to a bowl that's been greased with a little olive oil. Cover lightly with plastic wrap and let rest in a warm place (about 75°F is ideal) until doubled in size, about 1 hour. Use the dough immediately or keep it in the refrigerator for 24 hours, covered; let it come back to room temperature before using.

NOTE

Milk produces a softer dough, which I prefer for many of the recipes in this book, but water is more traditional.

Extra-Rich Short Pastry

The richness in this pastry adds extra flavor and depth, making it my go-to crust for pies and tarts with an elegant appeal. It's especially great for tart crusts that are prebaked because it tends to hold its shape well, without too much puffiness. When you first make the dough, expect it to be a little sticky. It's very rich and a bit wetter than the dough I use most often, but don't worry—it will become easier to handle once it has rested in the refrigerator.

To assemble a pie using this dough, it can be helpful to roll it between sheets of parchment paper or waxed paper.

MAKES TWO 8 TO 10-INCH PIE CRUSTS OR ONE 8 TO 10-INCH DOUBLE-CRUST SHELL

2¾ cups (390 grams) all-purpose flour, scooped and leveled, plus more as needed

1 teaspoon kosher salt

2 sticks (1 cup) plus 2 tablespoons very cold European-style (high-fat) butter, cut into ½-inch dice

1 large egg yolk, lightly beaten

2 tablespoons heavy cream

In the bowl of a food processor, pulse the 2 ¾ cups flour and the salt until well combined. Add the butter and egg yolk and continue pulsing until the mixture is crumbly and coarse, with various-size chunks of butter visible throughout.

With the machine running, add the cream through the feed tube a tablespoon at a time until the dough just comes together and begins to pull away from the sides, 15 to 20 seconds. You might not use all the cream. Don't overwork the dough, or the pastry will be tough. You'll notice that this dough is smoother and more homogenous than the Basic Pie Pastry (page 16). On a lightly floured work surface, gently knead the dough 2 or 3 times. If it seems quite sticky, sprinkle in another few teaspoons of flour and give it a couple more quick, gentle kneads. Divide in half and shape into 2 discs about 5 inches in diameter and ¾ inch thick, or as indicated in the individual recipe. Wrap in plastic and refrigerate at least 1 hour (or up to 2 days), or freeze for up to 1 month.

Gluten-Free Pie Pastry

MAKES TWO 8 TO 10-INCH PIE CRUSTS OR ONE 8 TO 10-INCH DOUBLE-CRUST SHELL

2 cups millet flour

¼ cup tapioca flour

¼ cup potato starch, plus more as needed

1 teaspoon salt

2 teaspoons lemon juice or white vinegar

2 sticks (1 cup) very cold European-style (high-fat) unsalted butter, cut into ½-inch dice

1 egg, lightly beaten

2 tablespoons water, or more as needed

In the bowl of a food processor, pulse the millet flour, tapioca flour, potato starch, and salt 5 or 6 times until well combined. Add the lemon juice or vinegar and butter. Process 6 to 8 seconds until crumbly and coarse, with various-size chunks of butter visible throughout. Add the egg and 2 tablespoons water. Run the machine until the dough comes together and begins to pull away cleanly from the sides of the bowl, 15 to 20 seconds. If this doesn't happen, add another few teaspoons water, as needed. Don't worry too much about overworking this dough, because there are no glutens to become tough. But don't let the dough get too wet.

On a work surface lightly floured with potato starch, gently knead the dough 2 or 3 times. If it seems quite sticky, sprinkle in another few teaspoons of potato starch and give it a couple more quick, gentle kneads. Divide in half and shape into 2 discs about 5 inches in diameter and ¾ inch thick, or as indicated in the individual recipe. Wrap in plastic and refrigerate at least 1 hour (or up to 2 days), or freeze for up to 1 month.

> **NOTE**
>
> Millet flour, tapioca flour, and potato starch are available in some specialty markets and health food stores.
>
> When choosing this gluten-free pastry for any of the pies in this book, you can substitute potato starch whenever the recipe specifies "flour for rolling."

APPETIZERS

Carrot and Leek Tarts with Aged Goat Cheese

You'll notice that in this recipe I specify aged goat cheese—different from the fresh goat cheese that has become known as chèvre in North America. I'm not saying you can't use the soft stuff, but if you take a little time to find the aged cheese (and, yes, spend a little more money), I think you'll see why I make the distinction. The carrots and leeks in this tart are caramelized to maximize their sweet, earthy flavors. Aged goat cheese brings just the right punchy, brackish contrast.

The goat cheeses of the Loire Valley are generally considered to be the standard bearers; Valençay is perhaps the most famous, with its unique flattened pyramid shape. But North America also makes some great aged goat cheeses. Vermont Creamery produces a version it calls Bonne Bouche that is indeed a good mouthful.

MAKES 6

Extra-Rich Short Pastry (page 19)*

6 teaspoons poppy seeds, divided

8 large carrots, peeled and cut into ¼-inch rounds

4 tablespoons olive oil, divided

Kosher salt and freshly cracked pepper

2 teaspoons mustard seeds

3 leeks (white and pale green parts), thinly sliced crosswise (about 8 ounces by weight after trimming and slicing)

1 teaspoon sugar

2 tablespoons white wine vinegar

1 tablespoon plus 1 teaspoon minced fresh flat-leaf parsley, divided

1 egg yolk

½ cup heavy cream

¼ cup finely grated Parmesan cheese

4 ounces aged goat cheese

* Other choices: Basic Pie Pastry (page 16), Cream Cheese Crust (page 17), and Gluten-Free Pie Pastry (page 20).

Prepare the dough for the crust and shape it into 2 discs about 5 inches in diameter and ¾ inch thick. Wrap in plastic and refrigerate at least 1 hour (or up to 2 days), or freeze for up to 1 month. Divide each chilled dough disc into 3 equal pieces; form into balls and use your thumb to press a well in the center of each. Pour 1 teaspoon poppy seeds into each well and pinch closed. Knead just enough to distribute the seeds, then roll into 6 rounds about 6 ½ inches in diameter and a generous ⅛ inch thick. (It can be helpful to roll this dough between sheets of parchment or waxed paper.)

Carefully transfer each round into a 4¾ to 5-inch round tart pan with removable bottom. Gently press to push the dough into the fluted sides, draping any excess over the sides; run a rolling pin over the top to trim. Patch any holes or tears, or the baked tarts may be hard to remove from the pans. Refrigerate until chilled, about 20 minutes.

Place an oven rack in the center position. Preheat the oven to 400°F.

Line each tart shell with parchment paper and fill with pie weights, copper pennies, dried beans, or rice. Place on a baking sheet and bake until set but not fully cooked, 12 to 14 minutes. Cool on a rack on the baking sheet; remove the parchment liners and weights. Reduce the oven temperature to 375°F.

In a medium bowl, toss the sliced carrots with 2 tablespoons olive oil and a big pinch each of salt and pepper. Spread on a parchment-lined baking sheet in as close to a single layer as possible; use a second baking sheet if necessary. Roast until the carrots begin to caramelize, about 18 minutes. Remove and let cool.

Heat the remaining 2 tablespoons olive oil in a medium saucepan over medium heat. Add the mustard seeds and cook until they begin to crackle and pop, about 2 minutes. Add the leeks and a pinch of salt. Cook, stirring often to separate the layers, until softened but not yet beginning to color, about 12 minutes. Stir in the sugar and vinegar and reduce the heat to low. Cook, stirring continuously, until the liquid has almost evaporated, about 1 minute. Remove from the heat, stir in 1 tablespoon parsley, and let cool.

In a medium bowl, whisk the egg yolk with the cream until frothy. Stir in the Parmesan and a pinch each of salt and pepper.

To assemble the tarts, spoon the leek mixture evenly among the shells, spreading it smooth. Spoon a scant 2 tablespoons cream mixture into each tart—don't let it overflow, or the tart will be hard to remove. Crumble goat cheese on top and then arrange carrot slices in slightly overlapping concentric circles, using as uniformly sized slices as possible. Save leftover slices for a salad or other dish.

🌿 WINE PAIRING

Sauvignon Blanc from the Loire Valley, preferably Sancerre or Pouilly-Fume.

Grassier and more herbal than the more tropical-style wines from New Zealand, these are in my opinion the world's purest examples of the variety. A crisp and dry Loire Valley Sauvignon Blanc with goat cheese is a classic pairing. The key for me is the distinct chalky minerality. Recommended producers: Guy Saget, Joseph Mellot, Domaine Laporte.

Sprinkle with the remaining 1 teaspoon parsley and a small pinch each of salt and pepper. Bake the tarts on the baking sheet until the filling has set, about 20 minutes. Let rest on a wire rack at least 10 minutes before removing the tart rings. Serve warm or at room temperature.

Prosciutto-Wrapped Fig Mini Pies

The prosciutto becomes beguilingly saltier as it bakes, and Gorgonzola provides some bite. But it's the figs that carry the weight in these little pies, so taste one first. If it's very ripe and very sweet, you may not need the honey.

MAKES 8

Basic Pie Pastry (page 16)

Flour for rolling

5 ounces shelled pecans, coarsely chopped

3 tablespoons olive oil, plus more for tins

½ teaspoon grated lemon zest

½ teaspoon minced fresh thyme leaves

Kosher salt and freshly cracked
   black pepper

8 whole figs, stem ends trimmed

8 slices prosciutto

4 ounces Gorgonzola cheese, crumbled

Honey, as needed (optional)

1 large egg yolk lightly beaten with
  1 teaspoon water, for egg wash

Prepare the pastry dough and shape it into two 5-inch squares about ¾ inch thick. Wrap in plastic and refrigerate at least 1 hour. On a lightly floured surface, use a lightly floured rolling pin to roll 1 chilled dough square to a bit bigger than a 10-inch square, a generous ⅛ inch thick. Trim the edges and cut into four 5 x 5-inch squares. Fit into the lightly greased cups of a standard-size muffin tin, leaving an even overhang all around. Repeat with the remaining dough. Refrigerate until chilled, about 20 minutes.

Meanwhile, place an oven rack in the center position. Preheat the oven to 400°F.

Place the nuts in the bowl of a food processor. With the processor running slowly, add olive oil until the mixture is finely chopped but not pasty; you may not use all the oil. Scrape into a small bowl, add the lemon zest and thyme, season to taste with salt and pepper, and stir to combine.

Divide the nut filling among the chilled pie crusts. Wrap each trimmed fig with a slice of prosciutto and place it in a muffin cup. Sprinkle with Gorgonzola, adding a small drizzle of honey if desired. Brush the exposed dough with egg wash. Place in the oven and immediately reduce the temperature to 375°F. Bake until the crusts are golden brown, the figs are quite soft, and the prosciutto is crisp, about 25 minutes.

Let cool completely in the tin on a wire rack. (These can also be made up to 24 hours ahead and kept at room temperature, covered.) Serve with a drizzle of honey, if you wish.

Spiced Chicken Pistachio Phyllo Triangles

I was inspired by the flavors of the Middle East when I developed this recipe, most particularly a Turkish-style lamb pizza known as lahmacun. *I've opted to use chicken thighs, however. They have a crumbly yet still chewy texture when prepared as described here, adding some heft to the satisfying multilayered crunch of phyllo folded into a traditional triangular shape.*

MAKES 36

8 ounces boneless, skinless chicken thighs

1 medium shallot, minced

1 clove garlic, minced

½ teaspoon kosher salt

1 teaspoon ground allspice

½ teaspoon ground cinnamon

½ teaspoon paprika

¼ teaspoon ground cloves

¼ teaspoon cayenne pepper, or to taste

2 tablespoons olive oil, plus more as needed

1 tablespoon minced fresh tarragon

1 teaspoon grated lemon zest

¼ cup finely chopped pistachios

¼ cup finely grated Parmesan cheese

Cooking spray (preferably olive oil) or melted butter, as needed

24 sheets purchased phyllo dough, thawed in the refrigerator

Minted Yogurt Dipping Sauce

1 cup plain yogurt

1 tablespoon lemon juice

1 clove garlic, chopped

½ teaspoon ground cumin

Pinch of kosher salt

½ cup loosely packed chopped fresh mint leaves

Roughly chop the chicken thighs. Place in the bowl of a food processor and pulse 8 to 10 times, until the texture resembles slightly wet, coarsely ground beef. Add the shallot, garlic, salt, allspice, cinnamon, paprika, cloves, and cayenne. Process about 15 seconds, until well combined and uniformly smooth in texture, almost like a paste.

Heat 2 tablespoons oil in a large skillet over medium-high heat. Add the chicken mixture and cook about 8 minutes, using a wooden spoon to break up the meat. When cooked through and uniformly crumbly, remove from the heat, adjust the seasoning if needed, and transfer to a fine-mesh sieve set over a bowl to drain and cool completely.

Return the cooled meat to the food processor bowl and process about 8 seconds, until uniformly grainy. Scrape into a bowl and mix in the tarragon, lemon zest, pistachios, and Parmesan.

Place racks in upper and center oven positions. Preheat the oven to 375°F.

Carefully unroll the phyllo pastry and transfer 24 sheets to a parchment-lined baking sheet. Cover loosely with plastic wrap and lay a barely damp kitchen towel on top to keep the phyllo from drying out as you work.

Stack 2 sheets of phyllo vertically on your work surface (re-cover the remaining sheets). Lightly spray the top sheet with cooking spray or brush with melted butter. With a knife, evenly cut the sheets in thirds lengthwise, leaving 3 piles of strips about 3 inches wide. Working with a single pile at a time, place about 1 tablespoon filling 2 inches up from the bottom left corner. Fold the bottom right corner up at a 45° angle to enclose the filling, forming 1 side of a triangle. Press to seal the edges. Continue folding as you'd fold a flag, alternating left and right to create a tight triangular bundle. Tuck the ends under and seal with more olive oil or butter. Lightly brush or spray exposed surfaces with more cooking spray or butter.

Repeat with the remaining phyllo and filling, placing the 36 filled triangles on 2 parchment-lined baking sheets. Bake until golden brown, about 12 to 15 minutes, switching the sheets halfway through.

For the Minted Yogurt Dipping Sauce, combine the yogurt, lemon juice, garlic, cumin, and salt in a blender. Blend at high speed until well incorporated, about 5 seconds. Lower the blender speed and slowly incorporate the mint until well chopped and distributed throughout. Transfer to a serving bowl to serve with the hot phyllo triangles. Can be made up to 1 day in advance.

Mushroom Tarte Tatin

The apple version of this classic supposedly was "invented" by a couple of clumsy French sisters named Tatin. Legend has it they either dropped the tart upside down on the floor or foolishly put it together the wrong way. We may never know the real story. But we do know that the dessert gained worldwide recognition when the très chic Maxim's Restaurant put it on the menu.

I've decided to turn dessert expectations upside down with a savory version featuring mushrooms and sweetly caramelized onions—a relatively simple preparation that comes across as obscenely posh. It makes an elegant first course, or the meaty mushrooms are satisfying enough that it can stand on its own as a vegetarian entrée.

MAKES 6

2 tablespoons unsalted butter, divided, plus more for the ramekins

Flour for rolling

1 (14-ounce) package frozen all-butter puff pastry, thawed in the refrigerator *

2 tablespoons olive oil, divided

4 large onions, halved and very thinly sliced with the grain

2 teaspoons minced fresh thyme leaves, divided, plus more for garnish

1 teaspoon kosher salt, plus more as needed

3 teaspoons sherry vinegar, divided

5 tablespoons water, divided

Freshly cracked black pepper

2 pounds assorted mushrooms (such as cremini, shitake, and chanterelles), thinly sliced

1 clove garlic, minced

¼ cup sugar

* Two sheets from a 17.3-ounce package of puff pastry can be stacked, folded, and rolled together as a substitute for the 14-ounce package listed above; you'll have pastry left over.

Butter six 4 to 5-ounce round ceramic or glass ramekins. Set aside.

On a lightly floured work surface, use a lightly floured rolling pin to roll the puff pastry to a rectangle about 10 x 15 inches, a scant ¼ inch thick. Use a cutter or template slightly larger than your ramekins (about 4 inches) to make 6 dough rounds. (Save the trimmings for another use.) Prick all over with a fork and transfer to a parchment-lined baking sheet. Refrigerate until chilled, about 20 minutes.

Melt 1 tablespoon butter with 1 tablespoon olive oil in a large skillet over medium heat. Once the foam subsides, add the onions, 1 teaspoon thyme, and 1 teaspoon salt. Cook, stirring often, until the onions are softened somewhat, about 6 minutes. Reduce the heat and continue to cook slowly, stirring occasionally, until the onions are well caramelized and very soft, about 50 minutes more depending on the water content of your onions. Add 1 teaspoon vinegar and 1 tablespoon water; stir and scrape any browned bits from the bottom of the pan until most of the liquid has evaporated, about 3 minutes. Repeat using another teaspoon vinegar and another tablespoon water; the onions should be a bit jammy. Season with salt and pepper and transfer to a bowl.

In the same skillet, melt the remaining 1 tablespoon butter with the remaining 1 tablespoon olive oil over medium-high heat. Add the mushrooms, garlic, and a pinch of salt. Cook, stirring occasionally, until the mushrooms have given off their liquid and begun to color, about 6 minutes. Remove from the heat and stir in the remaining 1 teaspoon thyme. Adjust the seasoning with salt and pepper, if needed. Set aside.

Place an oven rack in the center position. Preheat the oven to 425°F.

In a small saucepan, combine the sugar and remaining 3 tablespoons water. Cook over medium heat, watching closely and gently swirling the pan often until the sugar melts and begins to turn amber, about 7 minutes. Add the remaining 1 teaspoon vinegar and swirl to incorporate. Be careful—it may splatter. Let cool about 1 minute and then pour a teaspoonful into each ramekin.

After the caramel cools a bit, line each caramel-coated ramekin bottom with 6 or 8 overlapping mushroom slices in an attractive pattern. Divide the remaining mushrooms among the ramekins, packing them in tightly until they come about halfway up the sides; you may have extras.

Spoon in the onions, packing them so they come nearly to the top; you may have extras. Top each ramekin with a chilled pastry round, tucking in the edges. Use your hand to compress the ingredients flat and even with the rim.

Place on a rimmed baking sheet and bake until the crusts are puffed and golden, 15 to 20 minutes. Let stand 5 minutes, then run a knife around to loosen the pastry. Carefully invert onto individual serving plates. Garnish with thyme and serve immediately, as an appetizer or as an elegant side dish.

Tuna Wonton "Poke Pies"

A few years back on a trip along Hawaii's Kona Coast, I made an effort to introduce myself to authentic Hawaiian food. Poke is a raw fish preparation that represents the best of the traditional but is also friendly to modern influences and flavors. According to my research, poke has been eaten in the Islands longer than any other food. Captain James Cook was served a simple form of poke in Hawaii as far back as 1878.

Today poke can be found everywhere from high-end resorts to hole-in-the-wall eateries. It comes premade at the grocery store or lovingly prepared by home cooks. It's a must at Island celebrations— no luau would be complete without at least three or four poke choices. Why not make one of those choices "poke pie"?

MAKES 48

Cooking spray

12 (4-inch) wonton wrappers, cut into squared quarters

1 tablespoon minced fresh lemongrass (white inner parts only)

1 tablespoon peeled and grated ginger

1 clove garlic, minced

Juice of 2 limes

1 tablespoon unseasoned rice vinegar

2 tablespoons prepared wasabi

1 teaspoon chili oil

3 tablespoons vegetable oil

Pinch of kosher salt (optional)

10 ounces sashimi-grade tuna, well-chilled and cut into ⅓-inch dice

3 tablespoons minced red onion

3 tablespoons minced fresh chives

3 tablespoons tobiko (flying fish roe)*

2 tablespoons black sesame seeds

1 tablespoon chopped fresh seaweed (such as *ogo*), for garnish (optional)*

* Tobiko and fresh seaweed can be purchased in Asian and specialty stores.

Position a rack in the center of the oven. Preheat the oven to 350°F.

Turn four 12-portion mini muffin tins upside-down and coat the undersides lightly with cooking spray. (Work in batches if you have fewer tins.) Arrange wonton squares on the upside-down muffin cups so they drape uniformly and aren't touching. The shape you're after is not so much a bowl as a slightly sloped plate.

Place the tins on a large baking sheet and bake until the wrappers are crisp and golden, about 7 minutes. Let cool in place on the muffin tins. (The wonton crusts can be baked up to 3 days in advance and stored in an airtight container at room temperature.)

Place the lemongrass, ginger, garlic, lime juice, vinegar, wasabi, and chili oil in the bowl of a mini food processor or blender. With the machine running slowly, pour in the vegetable oil and process until a thick emulsification forms. (Alternatively, you can use a bowl, a whisk, and elbow grease.) Add a pinch of salt if needed, to taste. In a large bowl, gently fold together the diced tuna, red onion, chives, tobiko, and sesame seeds. Add the dressing a little at a time, gently folding until the fish mixture is coated but not overly wet.

🌿 **WINE PAIRING**

Spicy, dry to off-dry Alsatian Gewurztraminer.

Highly aromatic, with exotic fruit fragrances and flavors such as lychee and passion fruit, these are full-bodied, lush whites that feel sweeter than they are—which I think makes them pair well with mildly spicy Asian flavors, particularly ginger and lemongrass. Recommended producers: Sparr, Domaine Rémy Gresser, Zind Humbrecht.

(You won't use all the dressing; save it for another use.) Cover and refrigerate until chilled, about 20 minutes.

Arrange the wonton crusts on a serving plate. Place a heaping teaspoon of tuna poke in the center of each. Garnish with a bit of seaweed, if using, and serve while the poke is still cool.

NOTE

Choosing sustainable seafood can be confusing. Seafood Watch rates fresh, Pacific troll- or pole-caught albacore and bigeye tuna as "Best Choice."

Scallop and Crab Puffs with Spicy Cucumbers

The delicate scallop and crab filling in these hors d'oeuvres-size bites is lightly flavored with aromatic lemongrass. The puffs are wildly sophisticated but surprisingly easy to make. Your secret weapon is store-bought puff pastry. The quality of this recipe depends on that pastry, so buy the best you can. There are well-known brands that can disappoint, in my opinion. They're loaded with all sorts of mystery fat, so read the label. Look for a brand that uses only pure butter. I like Dufour, and my recipes are sized according to their 14-ounce package. Made with French butter, it's better, frankly, than anything I could make at home. Something magical happens as butter melts in well-prepared puff pastry. The water trapped within becomes steam, forcing the pastry upward into a million flaky layers you'd never have guessed were there when you rolled out the dough.

MAKES 32

6 ounces sea scallops

6 ounces lump crab meat, picked over to remove shells and rinsed

1 (3-inch) piece of fresh lemongrass

1 teaspoon grated lemon zest

2 tablespoons minced fresh chives

1 tablespoon minced fresh cilantro

1 tablespoon minced fresh mint, plus whole leaves for garnish

Kosher salt

White pepper

Flour for rolling

2 (14-ounce) packages frozen all-butter puff pastry, thawed in the refrigerator*

2 egg yolks mixed with 2 teaspoons water, for egg wash

   * Two sheets from a 17.3-ounce package of puff pastry can be stacked, folded, and rolled together as a substitute for each 14-ounce package listed above; you'll have pastry left over.

Spicy Cucumbers

½ cup water

2 tablespoons sugar

¼ teaspoon sea salt

¼ cup unseasoned rice vinegar

1 small shallot, minced

½ English cucumber, peeled, halved lengthwise, seeded, and thinly sliced crosswise

Pinch of red pepper flakes, or to taste

Soy Ginger Dipping Sauce

2 tablespoons finely chopped peeled fresh ginger

1 cup soy sauce

½ cup sugar

½ cup water

¼ cup unseasoned rice vinegar

Cut the scallops into ¼-inch dice and place in a large bowl with the crab.

Peel off the tough outer layers of lemongrass, then finely mince the light-colored interior to make about 2 teaspoons. Gently fold the lemongrass and lemon zest into the scallops and crab. Cover and refrigerate at least 4 hours but no longer than 12 hours.

Prepare the Spicy Cucumbers. Bring the ½ cup water to a boil in a small saucepan, remove from the heat, and add the sugar and sea salt, swirling to dissolve. Mix in the vinegar, shallot, cucumber, and red pepper. Cover and refrigerate at least 1 hour but no longer than 12 hours.

Add the chives, cilantro, and mint to the chilled scallop and crab mixture. Season with a pinch each of salt and white pepper, folding to incorporate.

On a lightly floured work surface, use a lightly floured rolling pin to roll 1 package of puff pastry to a bit bigger than 12 x 12 inches, a generous ⅛-inch thick. Use a ruler and a pizza cutter or sharp knife to cleanly trim to a 12-inch square, then cut into 16 pieces 3 x 3 inches. Place about ½ inch apart on a parchment-lined baking sheet. Repeat with the remaining package of puff pastry, giving you a total of 32 squares. Use a second lined baking sheet if necessary. Refrigerate until chilled, about 20 minutes. Place 1 heaping teaspoon prepared scallop and crab filling in the center of each chilled pastry square. Using your finger, moisten the edges with a bit of the egg wash. Fold 2 opposite corners over the filling and pinch firmly to seal. Repeat with the other corners, creating a neat little pyramid. Pinch gently to close the seams, maintaining the pyramid shape. Brush the exposed pastry lightly with more egg wash. Chill once more for about 20 minutes.

Place oven racks in upper and center positions. Preheat the oven to 425°F. Bake the puffs for 15 minutes, until they are golden brown; switch the sheets halfway through. Remove from the baking sheets and let cool on wire racks for 10 minutes.

Meanwhile, prepare the Soy Ginger Dipping Sauce. In a small bowl, stir together the ginger, soy sauce, sugar, water, vinegar, and salt until the sugar and salt are dissolved.

Garnish the baked puffs with mint leaves and serve warm along with Spicy Cucumbers and/or Soy Ginger Dipping Sauce.

Cotija Cheese Bocaditos with Charred Chiles

Cotija cheese is an aged cow's-milk cheese from Mexico. It has a strong, salty flavor—in fact, it has twice the salt content of Cheddar. On its own, it could politely be called an acquired taste, but don't let that put you off. There's magic in cotija when it's paired with strong flavors or mellowed somewhat by other cheeses. It's most often crumbled or grated as a topping for soups, salads, beans, enchiladas, and tacos. In fact, cotija is considered the Parmesan of Mexico.

MAKES 48

Cream Cheese Crust (page 17)*

1 teaspoon ground annatto or turmeric

⅛ teaspoon ground cumin (optional)

1 Anaheim chile

1 serrano chile

6 ounces cotija cheese, finely grated

6 ounces cream cheese, softened

1 egg, lightly beaten

1 tablespoon minced fresh cilantro leaves

Flour for rolling

* Other choices: Basic Pie Pastry (page 16),
Extra-Rich Short Pastry (page 19), and
Gluten-Free Pie Pastry (page 20).

Prepare the crust recipe, adding 1 teaspoon ground annatto or turmeric and ⅛ teaspoon ground cumin, if using, to the flour mixture. Shape into 2 discs about 5 inches in diameter and ¾ inch thick. Wrap in plastic and refrigerate at least 1 hour (or up to 2 days), or freeze for up to 1 month.

Heat a dry cast-iron or other heavy-bottomed skillet over medium-high heat to the point that you can't hold your hand above it for more than 3 seconds. Char the chiles in the skillet, turning with tongs until blackened on all sides. Place in a paper sack, close tightly, and let steam for about 10 minutes. Remove and rub off the blackened skin, being sure to wash your hands well afterward (wear rubber gloves if you're sensitive). Remove the stems and seeds, then mince about 1 tablespoon Anaheim and 1 teaspoon serrano, more if you want it spicier. Save the rest for another use.

In a medium bowl, stir together the minced chiles, cotija, and cream cheese. Add the egg and cilantro and mix until smooth. Set aside at least 30 minutes (or up to 2 days, refrigerated) for the flavors to meld.

Line 2 baking sheets or round pizza trays with parchment paper. On a lightly floured work surface, use a lightly floured rolling pin to roll 1 dough disc into a 15-inch round, less than ⅛ inch thick. Because the rolled dough is so thin, I like to fold it over the rolling pin and transfer it to a large pizza tray at this point. I can then cut it into twenty-four 2½-inch rounds right on the pizza tray, removing the scraps. But that's just an option. Either way, repeat with the rest of the chilled dough, giving you 48 rounds on 2 trays. Refrigerate until chilled, about 20 minutes.

Working with the dough rounds on their trays, place a scant 1 teaspoon of the chilled filling in the center of each round. (Don't overfill, or they'll be difficult to seal.) Moisten the edges with a little water, using your finger. Fold into half-moons so the edges meet; press together to seal. Use a small, sharp knife to make an X-shaped vent in the center of each bocadito. Cover and refrigerate until chilled, at least 20 minutes or up to 1 hour. (They can also be frozen, tightly covered in a single layer, for up to 1 month, then baked while still frozen.)

Meanwhile, place oven racks in upper and center positions. Preheat the oven to 375°F.

Bake the bocaditos until golden brown, about 25 minutes, switching the sheets halfway through. Remove from the baking sheets and let cool on wire racks for 10 minutes. Serve warm.

> **NOTE**
>
> If you are on a salt-restricted diet, or you prefer a milder flavor, you could replace the cotija cheese with ranchero cheese.

Garlic and Rosemary Pizzettes

The dough at the very best pizzerias has a yeasty, fermented quality that's hard to reproduce at home. That's because they often start the dough-making process with a yeast and flour mixture known as a "sponge." Typically, that sponge has been allowed to ferment for a period of time, producing superior flavor and texture. But I find that the less-involved Easy Flatbread Dough, and even good-quality purchased dough, can develop a similar slightly fermented taste if allowed to sit at room temperature for a couple of hours before the pie preparation begins.

MAKES 20

10 cloves garlic, divided

2 tablespoons olive oil, plus more for drizzling

1½ pounds Easy Flatbread Dough (page 18), or purchased pizza dough

cornmeal, as needed

1 ounce well-chilled low-moisture mozzarella cheese, shredded

1 tablespoon minced fresh rosemary, plus sprigs for garnish

1 ounce finely grated Parmesan cheese

Mince 5 cloves of the garlic. Heat 2 tablespoons olive oil in a small saucepan over medium-high heat. Add the minced garlic and cook, swirling the pan often, until it is sizzling and just beginning to color, about 2 minutes. Remove from the heat, and set aside to cool in the oil.

Divide the dough into 16 pieces the size of Ping-Pong balls (or slightly smaller). Flatten or roll each piece into a thin disc about 3½ inches in diameter. Place on a parchment-lined baking sheet lightly dusted with cornmeal. Don't crowd; you may need to use 2 baking sheets. Let rest at room temperature at least 20 minutes.

Place an oven rack in an upper position. Preheat the oven to 500°F or higher.

If the dough rounds have retracted after resting, use your fingertips to return them to about 3½-inch size. Brush with a little cooled garlic and olive oil mixture, getting plenty of crunchy garlic bits onto each piece. Divide the mozzarella evenly among the rounds, followed by minced rosemary and Parmesan.

Thinly slice the remaining 5 cloves of garlic. Garnish each pizzette with 2 or 3 garlic slices, a tiny sprig of rosemary, and a small drizzle of olive oil. Bake for 6 to 8 minutes, or until the crusts are golden and crisp and the cheese is getting slightly charred. Watch carefully, as they can go from charred to burnt quickly. Serve hot.

Tomato Caprese Tarts with Chive Oil

Caprese is a summertime treat that should only be made with the very best tomatoes. When the tomatoes are good, this traditional Italian salad with mozzarella and basil needs little in the way of condiments. But what happens the rest of the year? Do you just do without this classic combination of flavors? I say no way. Sweet 100 tomatoes are available on the vine at most major markets all year. They may not be quite the same as the ones you grow in your own backyard, but roasting them into this caprese-inspired tart amplifies their sweet nature.

MAKES 6

½ cup fresh chives, coarsely chopped

1 cup extra-virgin olive oil

Flour for rolling

2 (14-ounce) packages frozen all-butter puff pastry, thawed in the refrigerator*

3 ounces well-chilled low-moisture mozzarella cheese, coarsely shredded, divided

18 large cherry tomatoes or small Sweet 100s (on the vine, if possible)

Cooking spray

1 egg yolk lightly beaten with 1 teaspoon water, for egg wash

Kosher salt

Fresh whole basil leaves, for garnish

Aged balsamic vinegar

* Two sheets from a 17.3-ounce package of puff pastry can be stacked, folded, and rolled together as a substitute for each 14-ounce package listed above; you'll have pastry left over.

Bring to a boil a small saucepan half-filled with unsalted water. Add the chives and blanch for about 10 seconds; they should be very bright green. Drain in a colander and run cold water over them to stop the cooking. Pat dry with paper towels.

Put the chives and half the extra-virgin olive oil in a blender. With the machine running, add the remaining olive oil in a slow stream until completely puréed. Let the chive oil stand 1 hour and then strain through a fine-mesh sieve lined with a double thickness of damp cheesecloth. Discard the solids.

On a lightly floured work surface, use a lightly floured rolling pin to roll 1 package of puff pastry to a 10 x 15-inch rectangle, a scant ¼ inch thick. Use a 4-inch cutter to make 6 pastry rounds. Transfer to a parchment-lined baking sheet. On a freshly floured work surface, use a freshly floured rolling pin to roll the second package of puff pastry to a 10 x 15-inch rectangle, a scant ¼ inch thick. Use a cutter to cut 6 more 4-inch rounds. Then use a 3-inch cutter to cut out the centers of these rounds, creating rings. Save the trimmings for another use.

Brush the outside edges of the rounds with egg wash. Carefully lay the rings on top, aligning the edges. Use a fork to prick the pastry at half-inch intervals inside the raised border. Refrigerate until chilled, about 20 minutes.

Set an oven rack in the center position. Preheat the oven to 425°F.

Divide the mozzarella among the pastry rounds, about 2 tablespoons (½ ounce) each, keeping it inside the borders. Lay 3 tomatoes on top of the mozzarella; it's okay if they touch or overhang a little. Leave the vine attached or remove it, as you see fit. Give the tomatoes a spritz of cooking spray (preferably olive oil). Brush the tart edges with egg wash and sprinkle with a pinch of salt.

Bake until the pastry is golden and the tomatoes are just beginning to crack and blister, 15 to 20 minutes. Serve warm or at room temperature, garnished with lots of fresh basil leaves. Serve chive oil and balsamic vinegar on the side as a dressing.

Roasted Radish Tart with Arugula and Bagna Cauda

Radishes don't get a whole lotta love. Usually they get pushed around the salad bowl by diners in search of prettier pickings. They're the food equivalent of church lady chaperones at a high school dance—they always seem to be lurking but weren't really invited. But guess what? Radishes are just another root vegetable. There are many ways to love vegetables from the underworld, but roasting is just about my favorite. Parsnips, carrots, and beets are commonly roasted because it brings out their distinctive, rustic charm and bolsters the sugars. That got me thinking. Could I roast a radish?

MAKES 6 SLICES

Basic Pie Pastry (page 16)*

3 cloves garlic, coarsely chopped

4 anchovy fillets

2 tablespoons butter, at room temperature

4 tablespoons olive oil, divided

3 tablespoons freshly squeezed lemon juice

4 bunches radishes (just under 2 pounds)

Flour for rolling

6 cups arugula, loosely packed

Lemon wedges for spritzing

Freshly cracked black pepper

* Other choices: Cream Cheese Crust (page 17), Extra-Rich Short Pastry (page 19), and Gluten-Free Pie Pastry (page 20).

Prepare the pastry dough and shape it into 2 rectangles about 6 x 3 inches, about ¾ inch thick. Wrap in plastic and refrigerate at least 1 hour (or up to 2 days), or freeze for up to 1 month.

In a mini food processor or blender, pulse the garlic 10 or 12 times to uniformly chop. Add the anchovy fillets, butter, 2 tablespoons olive oil, and lemon juice. Process until you have a thick paste. Set aside.

Remove the tops and cut the radishes into quarters or halves, depending on size; you want the pieces to be fairly uniform. Leave very small ones whole. Trim neatly or leave on a bit of the stem end and most of the tail for a more rustic appearance, whichever you prefer.

Heat 1 tablespoon olive oil in a large skillet over medium-high heat. Add about half the radishes, cut sides down in as close to a single layer as possible. Cook undisturbed until the bottoms begin to caramelize, about 4 minutes. Then give the skillet a good shake and cook 2 or 3 minutes more, shaking the pan occasionally; transfer to a medium bowl. Repeat with the remaining 1 tablespoon olive oil and the rest of the radishes; add to the bowl. Reduce the burner heat and scrape the reserved bagna cauda paste into the skillet. Cook, stirring the whole time, until the mixture liquefies, about 1 minute. Pour over the radishes and toss to coat. Set aside.

On a lightly floured surface, use a lightly floured rolling pin to roll 1 chilled dough rectangle to about 16 x 6 inches, a generous ⅛ inch thick. (Save the rest of the dough for another use.)

Carefully fold in half crosswise, slide onto the rolling pin, and transfer to a 14 x 4-inch fluted tart pan with a removable bottom. Unfold, easing the dough into the tart pan. Gently press to line the pan without stretching the dough. Form neat corners, using gentle pressure to push the dough into the sides. Drape any excess over the sides and run a rolling pin across the top to trim. Patch any holes or tears, or the baked tart may be hard to remove. Generously prick the bottom with a fork. Refrigerate until chilled, about 20 minutes.

Place an oven rack in the center position. Preheat the oven to 375°F. Line the chilled tart crust with aluminum foil or parchment paper, allowing it to overhang all 4 sides by about 2 inches. Fill with pie weights, copper pennies, rice, or dried beans, spreading them to make sure the edges are supported. Place on a baking sheet and bake until just beginning to color, about 14 minutes.

Remove from the oven and lift out the liner and pie weights. Pour in the radishes and accumulated sauce in a heaping mound, filling the entire shell. Return to the hot oven and bake until the radishes are tender-crisp and the crust is golden brown, about 30 minutes.

Let cool on a rack at least 10 minutes before removing the tart mold. Slice into 6 portions and top each with arugula, a spritz of lemon, and a good grind of black pepper.

Bite-Size Beef Wellingtons

I'm not really a gadget guy, though there are a few essential tools I recommend for every cook: chef's knife, pepper mill, colander, whisk, vegetable peeler, and iPad. I'd also put an instant-read thermometer on that list; in fact, it's the only kitchen tool I've been known to bring to dinner parties. It's super handy for answering that age-old question, "Is it done yet?" An instant-read thermometer takes away the guesswork: 125°F for medium-rare beef, 140°F for medium pork, 160° F for well-done poultry.

MAKES 6

2 pounds beef tenderloin, cut into 24 (1½-inch) cubes

½ teaspoon kosher salt, plus more as needed

¼ teaspoon freshly cracked black pepper, plus more as needed

¼ cup (½ stick) unsalted butter

¾ pound cremini or white button mushrooms, cut into ⅛-inch dice

¼ cup minced shallot

2 tablespoons minced fresh thyme leaves

2 cloves garlic, minced

½ cup vermouth or vegetable broth

¼ teaspoon truffle oil (optional)

Flour for rolling

1 (14-ounce) package frozen all-butter puff pastry, thawed in the refrigerator*

1 large egg yolk lightly beaten with 1 teaspoon water, for egg wash

Minced fresh chives, for garnish

* Two sheets from a 17.3-ounce package of puff pastry can be stacked, folded, and rolled together as a substitute for the 14-ounce package listed above; you'll have pastry left over.

In a medium bowl, toss the beef cubes with ½ teaspoon salt and ¼ teaspoon pepper. Set aside.

Melt the butter in a medium saucepan over medium heat. Add the mushrooms and cook, stirring occasionally, until they begin to brown and release their liquid, about 5 minutes. Add the shallots, thyme, and garlic. Cook, stirring occasionally, until the shallots soften, about 5 minutes more. Pour in the vermouth or vegetable broth and cook, stirring occasionally, until the moisture has nearly evaporated and the mushrooms are well browned, 10 to 12 minutes. Remove from the heat, adjust the seasoning with salt and pepper if needed, and stir in the truffle oil, if using. Set aside to cool.

On a lightly floured work surface, use a lightly floured rolling pin to roll the puff pastry to a rectangle about 10 x 15 inches, a scant ¼ inch thick. Trim neatly to a 10-inch square;

save the trimmings for another use. Cut crosswise into five 2-inch strips, then cut each strip into five 2-inch squares. You should have 25 squares.

Lightly coat the cups of two 12-portion mini muffin tins with cooking spray. Gently press a pastry square into each compartment. You'll have 1 square left over; save it with the trimmings for another use. Refrigerate until chilled, about 20 minutes.

Scoop 1 heaping teaspoon mushroom filling in each chilled pastry cup, followed by 1 beef cube. Cover with plastic wrap and refrigerate until chilled, about 20 minutes.

Place an oven rack in the center position. Preheat the oven to 425°F.

When ready to bake, brush the exposed dough with egg wash. Sprinkle with salt. Place the tins on a baking sheet and bake 12 to 15 minutes, until the pastry is puffed and golden and the meat is cooked to 125°F for medium-rare, more if you prefer medium. Let cool slightly. Carefully remove the pastry cups from the tins while still somewhat hot. Garnish with minced chives and serve warm.

❧ WINE PAIRING

Red Bordeaux, preferably from the Left Bank.

With aromas and flavors of black fruits, spice, and dusty earth, Bordeaux is great with beef. The wine's tannins are counter-balanced by the beef's fat and proteins, enhancing both the food and the wine. Also, the wine's earthiness complements the mushroom filling. Look for something from the excellent '09 vintage. Recommended producers: Château Lilian Ladouys, Château Cantemerle, Château Tour Seran.

Caviar and Quail's-Egg Tiny Tarts

The best way to eat good caviar is as simply as you can—the better the caviar, the fewer the accompaniments. Unfortunately, centuries of demand have demolished the fisheries of the species that produce the very best roe, sending the most prized fish from the Caspian Sea to the brink of extinction. For me, this has meant years of caviar-less Valentine's Day celebrations. There's nothing romantic about extinction. Many chefs and other palate influencers in the U.S. and Europe have turned their backs on wild caviar; the best way to get businesses to change their practices is to quit buying their products. Sure enough, caviar suppliers felt the pinch and have begun producing an acceptable alternative in the form of farm-raised organic American sturgeon caviar. So check the label and indulge yourself once in a while.

MAKES 32

½ cup white vinegar

2 cups water

16 quail eggs

2 tablespoons minced fresh chives, plus more for garnish

¼ teaspoon white pepper

¾ cup crème fraîche

32 prebaked purchased tiny tart shells (approximately 1¾-inch)

4 ounces farm-raised organic American sturgeon caviar, chilled

Pour the vinegar and water into a medium saucepan. Carefully place the quail eggs in the water and turn the heat to high. As soon as the water comes to a boil, turn off the heat and cover the pan. Don't be alarmed if the spots come off the egg shells. Leave covered for 4 minutes.

Fill a medium bowl with cool water and immerse the eggs to stop the cooking process. When cool enough to handle, crack the shells by tapping them on the edge of the bowl, then gently peel. The vinegar makes the shells quite pliable. Set aside. (This can be done up to 8 hours ahead; keep covered and chilled.)

In a small bowl, stir together the chives, white pepper, and crème fraîche until well incorporated. Set aside. (This can be done up to 8 hours ahead; keep covered and chilled.) Before serving, bring the caviar, eggs, and crème fraîche mixture to room temperature, about 15 minutes. Slice the eggs in half lengthwise. Arrange the tart shells on a serving platter or individual plates. Spoon a generous teaspoon of crème fraîche mixture into each shell, snuggle a half-egg next to it, and dollop about ½ teaspoon caviar on top. Garnish with minced chives. Serve immediately.

Pesto Trapanese Muffin-Tin Pies

The Italian city of Trapani on Sicily's westernmost tip has an identity all its own. Geographically speaking, it's closer in both distance and topography to Tunis than it is to Naples. In fact, it's closer to several African ports than to any part of mainland Italy. Almonds are a rather frequent ingredient in the cooking of Trapani (and Sicily in general). They grow all over the place, and it's not unusual to see almond trees growing in the wild alongside date and citrus trees. They all found their way to Sicily on ancient trading ships and have established themselves quite nicely.

My favorite of the almond-centric dishes is the Trapanese version of pesto. I'm sure the Genovese might argue with the term "pesto," as this sauce isn't green at all. It's a rustic mix of chopped almonds, garlic, basil, and cherry tomatoes. There's often a bit of heat in the form of red pepper. Like a more traditional pesto, this Sicilian classic is traditionally pounded together in a mortar and pestle before being tossed with good local pasta. But I've decided to adapt it as the basis for the filling of an appetizer-size pie.

MAKES 8

Basic Pie Pastry (page 16)*

Flour for rolling

1 pound small cherry tomatoes

½ cup unsalted almonds, lightly toasted

¼ cup finely grated Parmesan cheese

1 teaspoon minced garlic

15 large basil leaves, coarsely chopped

¼ teaspoon red pepper flakes, or to taste

¼ cup olive oil, or as needed, plus more for the muffin tins

Kosher salt and freshly cracked black pepper

2½ ounces low-moisture mozzarella cheese, chilled and coarsely shredded

1 large egg yolk lightly beaten with 1 teaspoon water, for egg wash

* Other choices: Cream Cheese Crust (page 17), Extra-Rich Short Pastry (page 19), and Gluten-Free Pie Pastry (page 20).

Prepare the pastry dough and shape it into 2 squares about 5 inches across and ¾ inch thick. Wrap in plastic and refrigerate at least 1 hour (or up to 2 days), or freeze for up to 1 month.

On a lightly floured surface, use a lightly floured rolling pin to roll 1 chilled dough square a bit bigger than 10 inches square, a generous ⅛ inch thick. Trim the edges neatly and cut into four 5-inch squares. Lightly oil 8 cups of a standard-size muffin tin and fit in the dough squares, letting them hang over evenly all around. Repeat with the remaining dough, giving you 8 dough-lined cups. Refrigerate until chilled, about 20 minutes.

Place an oven rack in the center position. Preheat the oven to 400°F.

Set aside 24 of the nicest-looking cherry tomatoes. Cut the rest into quarters.

Place the almonds in the bowl of a food processor and pulse 15 to 20 times until coarsely chopped. Add the quartered tomatoes, Parmesan, garlic, basil, and red pepper. Pulse 8 or 10 times. With the machine running, pour the olive oil in a slow, steady stream through the feed tube. The resulting pesto should be quite grainy but not too chunky or wet; you may not need all the oil. Adjust the seasoning with a pinch each of salt and pepper, if necessary.

Dollop a heaping tablespoon of pesto into each dough-lined muffin cup. (You may have some left over to toss with cooked pasta as the cook's reward.) Place 3 of the reserved tomatoes in each cup and sprinkle about 1 tablespoon mozzarella on top. Fold the overhanging dough corners inward to cover loosely and attractively. They don't need to meet in the center or be perfectly flat; create ruffles and folds for the best result. Brush the exposed dough with egg wash and sprinkle with salt.

Bake until the crusts are golden brown and the whole tomatoes are quite soft, about 25 minutes. Let the tin cool on a rack for about 5 minutes and then remove the pies to serve warm. (These can also be made up to 24 hours ahead. In which case let come to room temperature before covering and refrigerating. To serve, gently reheat in the muffin tins for 10 minutes in a 300°F oven.)

NOTE

These can also be made in mini muffin tins to serve as hors d'oeuvres. Cut each large dough square into 24 small squares, 2 x 2 inches, and fill with 1 teaspoon pesto, 1 teaspoon mozzarella, and a single whole cherry tomato. Cooking time varies—watch closely.

Lamb and Apricot Phyllo Cups

Working with phyllo can be a little fussy, and even be a bit fear-inducing. I avoided it for years, dead sure my clumsy fingers lacked the necessary nimbleness. But as with most things in life, it turns out that this isn't nearly as hard as it looks. It is a little fussy, but that can be overcome with a few basic techniques. To keep the dough supple and moist, unfold or unroll the sheets and immediately cover them with plastic wrap and a barely damp kitchen towel. The biggest obstacle to success comes from dry, brittle sheets that just won't do what you ask them to. Work quickly and in small batches.

Most recipes have you build your layers with some sort of fat in between. I like butter best—it imparts richness, flavor, and a delicate crispness. But olive oil sprayed across each layer is a simple alternative. Still fearful? Don't fret—you can use premade frozen phyllo cups from the grocery store.

MAKES 48

4 sheets phyllo dough	8 ounces ground lamb
2 tablespoons butter, melted	1 teaspoon ground cumin
1 tablespoon vegetable oil	3 ounces dried apricots, finely chopped
½ cup finely chopped onion	2 ounces toasted pine nuts
2 cloves garlic, minced	¼ teaspoon red pepper flakes
½ teaspoon kosher salt, divided, or more as needed	4 tablespoons julienned fresh mint leaves, divided
⅛ teaspoon freshly cracked black pepper	3 ounces crumbled feta (optional)

For the phyllo cups, place an oven rack in the center position. Preheat the oven to 375°F.

Stack the phyllo sheets flat on a cutting board. Using a very sharp knife and a straightedge, trim to a 12 x 16-inch rectangle. Cut into 2-inch squares, 48 in all. Cover completely with plastic wrap and top with a barely damp kitchen towel. Pull out only as many squares as you can work with at one time.

Lightly brush the cups of four 12-portion mini muffin tins with butter. (Work in batches if you have fewer tins.) Mold a single-layer phyllo square in the bottom of a muffin cup and brush lightly with more butter. Follow with 3 more squares, altering positions slightly to create a fringed edge and brushing butter between layers. Repeat to form a total of 48 phyllo cups. Don't worry if the squares tear or fold—they'll form a solid cup once baked.

Bake until crisp and lightly golden, about 5 minutes. Let cool on a wire rack before removing from the tins. Set the cooled cups on several layers of paper towels to absorb excess butter. (The cups can be made up to 3 days ahead and stored airtight at room temperature.)

For the filling, heat the vegetable oil in a medium cast-iron or other heavy-bottomed skillet over medium heat. Add the onions, garlic, ¼ teaspoon salt, and ⅛ teaspoon pepper. Cook until the onions have softened somewhat, about 4 minutes. Add the lamb and cumin; cook, breaking up the meat with a wooden spoon, until browned and crumbly, about 10 minutes. Remove from the heat and stir in the apricots, pine nuts, red pepper, 2 tablespoons mint, and remaining ¼ teaspoon salt or more, to taste.

(The filling can be prepared the day before, without the 2 tablespoons mint or final ¼ teaspoon salt, and refrigerated. At assembly time, gently reheat with a teaspoon of water. Add the mint and salt once the mixture is at serving temperature.)

To assemble, place a heaping teaspoon of lamb filling in each phyllo cup. Garnish with a few strips of julienned mint and a bit of feta, if using. Serve warm.

You can also fill the cups up to 1 hour ahead, without the garnish. Warm them in a 300°F oven for 5 minutes. Sprinkle on the mint and feta, if using, just before serving.

MAIN COURSE PIES— MEATS AND SEAFOOD

Classic Chicken Pot Pies

When I was a kid, chicken pot pies came into our house frozen. They came in only one shape and size, their edges decorated with perfect little hatch marks, each pie exactly like the others—no fighting over who got the best one. They were served hot as magma in mini aluminum pie pans, right before the babysitter arrived. Chicken pot pies were a convenience for my parents on nights when they were going out, so my mom was usually pulling them from the oven all dressed up like a movie star. Those pies (and those times) were like a drug to me, guaranteed to make me giddy with excitement. Here's the closest I could get to that feeling again.

MAKES 8 SERVINGS

Basic Pie Pastry (page 16)*

1 tablespoon plus 2 teaspoons minced fresh thyme leaves, divided

4 chicken breast halves, bone in and skin on (about 3 pounds)

Kosher salt and freshly cracked black pepper

¼ cup (½ stick) unsalted butter

½ large onion, diced into ¼-inch pieces (about 1 cup)

2 stalks celery, sliced into ¼-inch pieces (about 1 cup)

2 medium carrots, peeled and sliced into ¼-inch rounds (about 1 cup)

½ cup all-purpose flour, plus more for rolling

3 cups chicken broth

1 cup whole milk

1 cup frozen peas

2 tablespoons minced fresh flat-leaf parsley

1 tablespoon white vinegar

2 egg yolks lightly beaten with 2 teaspoons water, for egg wash

* Other choices: Cream Cheese Crust (page 17), Extra-Rich Short Pastry (page 19), and Gluten-Free Pie Pastry (page 20).

Prepare the pastry recipe, adding 1 tablespoon thyme to the flour mixture. Shape into 2 discs about 5 inches in diameter and ¾ inch thick. Wrap in plastic and refrigerate at least 1 hour (or up to 2 days), or freeze for up to 1 month.

Divide each chilled dough disc into 4 equal portions. On a lightly floured surface, use a lightly floured rolling pin to roll into each portion into a 6-inch round, a generous ⅛ inch thick. Lay the 8 rounds on a parchment-lined baking sheet, cover with plastic wrap, and refrigerate until chilled, at least 20 minutes or up to 8 hours.

Place an oven rack in the center position. Preheat the oven to 375°F.

Lay the chicken breasts skin-side up on a rimmed, parchment-lined baking sheet.

Season generously with salt and pepper and then roast until cooked through, about 35 minutes. Set aside to cool somewhat. Remove the skin (It's okay to eat it while no one's looking). Strip the meat from the bones, cutting it into bite-size chunks. You should have about 5½ cups roasted chicken.

Melt the butter in a medium saucepan over medium heat. Add the onions and a big pinch each of salt and pepper. Cook until softened, stirring often, about 4 minutes. Add the celery and carrots; cook until softened, stirring occasionally, about 6 more minutes. Sprinkle in the ½ cup flour and cook another minute, stirring to combine. Gradually pour in the broth and milk, whisking until thickened, about 4 minutes. Add the chicken, peas, minced parsley, vinegar, and remaining 2 teaspoons thyme. Remove from the heat. Adjust the seasoning as needed with salt and pepper. Allow to cool completely.

Fill 8 mini pie tins or 1-cup ovenproof bowls or ramekins with the cooled chicken mixture. Brush the rims with egg wash.

Remove the dough rounds from the refrigerator and wait a bit for the dough to become pliable, then top each pie with a dough round. You can let the dough drape over the sides or trim and decorate the edge, as you like. Brush the tops with egg wash and sprinkle lightly with kosher salt. Use a sharp knife to cut 3 or 4 slits in a decorative pattern in each crust. Place on a rimmed baking sheet and bake until the tops are golden brown and the filling is bubbling, about 45 minutes. Let rest about 5 minutes before serving, hot as magma.

Sweet Sausage Cabbage Pie with Dill and Feta

This pie seems extra warm and cozy, so I don't need to say much. You can easily imagine the flavor combination—the sharp cheese teasing the sweet fennel into focus. Besides, nothing says comfort like cabbage baked in the oven—especially when that cabbage is wrapped in a flaky crust. This is the most casual of pies. The pastry comes together effortlessly. It rolls out beautifully, no crimping or fussy latticework involved. Simply line a gratin dish for the most straightforward presentation possible.

MAKES 4 SERVINGS

Basic Pie Pastry (page 16)*

¼ cup plus 2 tablespoons chopped fresh dill, divided

1 pound sweet Italian sausages

1 teaspoon fennel seeds

½ teaspoon kosher salt, plus more as needed

½ cabbage, cored and shredded slaw-style (about 6 cups, loosely packed)

1 tablespoon olive oil, or as needed

1 large onion, halved and sliced into slivers

2 cloves garlic, minced

Freshly cracked black pepper

5 ounces crumbled feta cheese, divided

¼ cup chopped fresh flat-leaf parsley

Flour for rolling

1 large egg yolk lightly beaten with 1 teaspoon water, for egg wash

* Other choices: Cream Cheese Crust (page 17), Extra-Rich Short Pastry (page 19), and Gluten-Free Pie Pastry (page 20).

Prepare the pastry recipe, adding 2 tablespoons dill to the flour mixture. Shape the dough into 2 discs about 5 inches in diameter and ¾ inch thick. Wrap in plastic and refrigerate at least 1 hour (or up to 2 days), or freeze for up to 1 month.

Remove the sausages from their casings. Discard the casings and crumble the meat; set aside. Set a large cast-iron or other heavy-bottomed skillet over medium-high heat. Add the fennel seeds and toast until fragrant, shaking the skillet often, about 2 minutes. Add the crumbled meat to the skillet. Lower the heat to medium. Cook, breaking up with a wooden spoon, until well browned, 10 to 12 minutes. Use a slotted spoon to move the meat to a plate; set aside.

Bring a large pot of generously salted water to a boil. Add the cabbage and blanch for 2 minutes. Drain in a colander, allow to cool for a couple of minutes, and dry—a salad spinner works well.

Set the skillet you used for the meat over medium heat. Add about 1 tablespoon oil to bring the total fat in the pan to about 2 tablespoons. Add the onion and cook, stirring often, until tender, about 6 minutes. Add ½ teaspoon salt and the garlic. Cook, stirring, until fragrant, about 1 more minute. Stir in the cooked meat and then add the blanched cabbage. Cook, stirring often, until the mixture is very tender and the cabbage is beginning to color, about 15 minutes. Add a generous grind of black pepper. Allow to cool somewhat. Stir in 3 ounces of feta, the remaining ¼ cup dill, and the parsley. Set aside to cool completely.

Place an oven rack in the center position. Preheat the oven to 375°F.

On a lightly floured surface, use a lightly floured rolling pin to roll a chilled dough disc to about a 13-inch round (depending on your baking dish), a generous ⅛ inch thick; save the second disc for another use. Carefully fold the rolled dough in half, slide onto the rolling pin, and transfer to a 10 x 7 x 2-inch-deep oval baking dish. Unfold, easing the dough gently into the dish and letting it drape evenly over the long sides without stretching. Fill to heaping with cabbage and sausage mixture and sprinkle with the remaining 2 ounces of feta. Fold the dough edges loosely over the filling; they don't have to meet in the center. Brush the exposed dough with egg wash, drizzling any extra over the cabbage mixture.

Place on a rimmed baking sheet and bake until the crust is crisp and dark golden brown, 40 to 50 minutes. Serve hot, warm, or at room temperature.

Mini Lamb Pies "Champvallon"

According to the Larousse Gastronomique, *this potato-topped French classic dates from the reign of Louis XIV. Supposedly it was invented by one of his mistresses. But which one? There are fourteen (quatorze!) officially recognized mistresses. The French call this dish Cotes d'agneau Champvallon, but I can find no reference to any of Louis' ladies with the name Champvallon. Since its origins are obscure, I've given myself license to tweak this recipe a bit—something more suited to the modern palate and served in cute little mini pie pans, the likes of which Louis XIV never saw.*

MAKES 8

½ cup plus 1 tablespoon all-purpose flour, divided

Kosher salt and freshly cracked pepper

3 pounds boneless lamb shoulder, cut into bite-size pieces

2 tablespoons olive oil, plus more as needed

2 onions, halved and thinly sliced

4 garlic cloves, thinly sliced

4 cups chicken broth

1 tablespoon minced fresh rosemary leaves, plus more for garnish

4 small russet potatoes (about 2½ inches in diameter), peeled

Place an oven rack in the center position. Preheat the oven to 300°F.

In a small, shallow bowl, mix ½ cup flour with a generous pinch each of salt and pepper. Roll the lamb pieces in the flour to coat; transfer them to a large plate as you work. Heat 2 tablespoons olive oil in a large Dutch oven over medium-high heat. Working in batches, brown the lamb about 2 minutes per side and return to the plate. Add more oil if necessary until all the pieces are browned.

Reduce the heat to medium and add more olive oil to the pot if it's dry. Add the onion and cook, stirring often, until it begins to color, about 8 minutes. Add the garlic and cook until fragrant, about 1 minute. Sprinkle in the remaining 1 tablespoon flour and cook, stirring the whole time, about 1 minute. Slowly add the chicken broth and rosemary, stirring and scraping the bottom to loosen any browned bits. Turn off the heat and return the lamb to the pot, stirring to incorporate. Cover with a tightly fitting lid and transfer to the oven. Braise until the meat is fork tender, about 2½ hours.

Divide the cooked filling among 8 mini pie pans or 1-cup casseroles or gratin dishes. Fill all the way to the top without heaping. You may need to add about a teaspoon of water to each pie to assure a good amount of sauce.

Raise the oven temperature to 375°F. Very thinly slice the potatoes crosswise into rounds; a mandolin works best for this. Arrange the slices over the lamb in a tight circle, overlapping the edge all the way around; it's fine if there's an opening in the center. Brush with olive oil, sprinkle with salt and pepper, and garnish with more rosemary. Place on a rimmed baking sheet and bake until the filling is bubbling and the potato crust is golden and beginning to curl, about 40 minutes (depending on the thickness of the potatoes). Let the pies rest on a rack for about 10 minutes. Serve hot.

🍷 WINE PAIRING

Young red wines from the northern Rhône Valley, preferably Crozes-Hermitage.

Made from Syrah grapes, these wines are typically well balanced with juicy red fruit flavors, leathery and peppery notes, and plenty of tangy acidity. With similar robust and earthy flavors, braised lamb and Rhône reds are natural partners. Recommended producers: Gilles Robin, Domaine du Colombier, Cave de Tain.

Braised Short Rib "Neeps and Tatties" Shepherd's Pie

"Neeps and tatties"—that phrase didn't spring out of my brain. It seems that neeps and tatties are a traditional Scottish combination. I'm sure you can guess that the "tatties" are taters (actually potaters), but "neeps" may be new to you. If so, I hope the name makes you smile as much as it does me. Neeps are a sort of Scottish turnip, or what we in North America might call a rutabaga. I can't take any credit for the classic combination of beef and Guinness in this neeps and tatties–topped shepherd's pie, either. It's a pie for the ages. Usually it's made with some cut of steak, but I prefer slow-braised beef short ribs because they elevate the comfort level to pure cush.

MAKES 8 SERVINGS

4 slices bacon

½ cup all-purpose flour, or more as needed

1 tablespoon mustard powder

Kosher salt and freshly cracked black pepper

4½ pounds bone-in beef short ribs, cut into 4-inch pieces

1 medium onion, coarsely chopped (about 2 cups)

2 stalks celery, coarsely chopped (about 1 cup)

2 medium parsnips or carrots, peeled and coarsely chopped (about 1 cup)

1 bay leaf

6 cloves garlic, coarsely chopped

1 pint Guinness stout*

3 cups beef broth

1 tablespoon Worcestershire sauce

2 tablespoons minced fresh thyme leaves

2 cups frozen pearl onions

2 pounds russet potatoes, peeled and cut into 2-inch chunks

1 pound rutabaga, peeled and cut into 1-inch chunks

3 tablespoons unsalted butter, divided

* Note: One way to buy Guinness stout in North America is in pint-plus-6-ounce bottles. That means there are 6 ounces left over for the cook to enjoy. Perfect.

Place an oven rack in a lower position. Preheat the oven to 300°F. Cook the bacon in a large cast-iron or other heavy-bottomed Dutch oven over medium heat, stirring occasionally, until it begins to brown and most of the fat has been rendered, 6 to 8 minutes. Remove with a slotted spoon, transfer to paper towels to drain, and then crumble or coarsely chop. Set aside. Discard all but about 2 tablespoons of the bacon fat. In a shallow bowl, mix the flour, mustard, and a generous pinch each of salt and pepper. Roll the meat chunks in the flour until well coated. Transfer to a large plate.

Raise the heat under the bacon fat to medium-high. When it's hot but not yet smoking, quickly brown the ribs on all three meaty sides, about 1 minute per side. Don't crowd the pot; work in batches if necessary. Transfer the cooked pieces to a large plate.

Once the meat has browned, reduce the heat to medium. Add the onions, celery, parsnips or carrots, and bay leaf to the pot; stir to coat. Cook, stirring occasionally, until the vegetables begin to soften, about 6 minutes. Stir in the garlic and 3 tablespoons of the remaining flour mixture; cook 1 more minute. Add the Guinness, scraping up any browned bits from the bottom.

Return the bacon and browned beef to the pot along with any accumulated juices. Add the beef broth, Worcestershire, and thyme. Cover with a tight-fitting lid and transfer to the oven. Braise until the beef is fork tender, 2½ to 3 hours.

Turn off the oven, remove the meat from the pot, and let it come to room temperature. Strain the sauce into a large saucepan, pressing down on the solids to extract as much flavor as possible; discard the solids. Set the saucepan over medium heat to reduce the sauce by a third, about 30 minutes. Skim off any fat and scum that come to the surface.

Meanwhile, chop the cooled meat into manageable bites, discarding bones, connective tissue, and any bits that don't appeal to you. Add the chopped meat to the saucepan along with the pearl onions. Cover and cook another 30 minutes, occasionally breaking up the meat with a wooden spoon. Transfer to a deep 2-quart baking dish. Let cool. (At this point the dish can be refrigerated, covered, for up to 3 days; in fact, it will benefit from resting at least overnight.) Skim or peel off the fat.

Place the potatoes, rutabagas, and 2 teaspoons salt in a large stockpot. Add just enough water to cover by about 1 inch. Bring to a boil, then reduce to a simmer. Cover and cook until the potatoes and rutabagas fall apart when poked with a fork, 20 to 25 minutes. Strain and then return half to the hot, dry pot. Reduce the heat to low and cook, uncovered, shaking the pan often to evaporate as much water as possible, about 4 minutes. Transfer to a large bowl. Repeat with the remaining potatoes and rutabagas. Let cool somewhat, then push through a ricer into a medium bowl. (Alternatively, you can use a masher or fork.) Beat in 2 tablespoons butter until smooth and creamy. Season to taste with salt and pepper.

Place an oven rack in the center position and preheat the oven to 375°F. Top the braised meat and its sauce with the potato and rutabaga purée. Dot lightly with the remaining 1 tablespoon butter. Place on a rimmed baking sheet—the sauce likely will bubble over. Bake until the top is browned in spots, 45 to 50 minutes. Serve hot.

Tuscan Kale and Pancetta Pie

Tuscan kale. That's quite a romantic moniker for such a healthy, leafy green vegetable, don't you think? The name may even be partly responsible for the fact that this cruciferous crusader is developing a bit of a cult status among chefs. It has a more delicate leaf with a less fibrous stem than the curly stuff you may be used to seeing. When I first saw Tuscan kale in the market a few years back, I was attracted by its pebbly, dark greenish blue leaves. This is an Italian variety that thankfully grows very well in the "Mediterranean" climate of southern California, where I live, but it's becoming popular the world over. I've also seen it referred to as black kale, lacinato, and dinosaur kale—presumably because of its reptilian, crenulated texture.

MAKES 6 TO 8 SERVINGS

Basic Pie Pastry (page 16)*

3 ounces finely grated Parmesan cheese, plus ½ ounce for crust (optional)

Kosher salt

2 pounds Tuscan kale, stems and thick veins removed (about 1½ pounds trimmed)

1 tablespoon olive oil

½ pound pancetta or slab bacon, sliced about ⅓ inch thick and cut into 1-inch lardons

2 cloves garlic, minced

1 large onion, cut into ¼-inch dice (about 2 cups)

2 large eggs, lightly beaten

15 ounces ricotta, drained

2 teaspoons fresh oregano leaves, minced

½ teaspoon freshly cracked black pepper, plus more as needed

½ cup lightly toasted pine nuts

¼ teaspoon red pepper flakes (optional)

Flour for rolling

1 egg yolk lightly beaten with 1 teaspoon water, for egg wash

* Other choices: Cream Cheese Crust (page 17), Extra-Rich Short Pastry (page 19), and Gluten-Free Pie Pastry (page 20).

Prepare the pastry recipe, adding ½ ounce Parmesan to the flour mixture, if you wish. Divide the dough in half and shape into 2 discs ¾ inch thick–one about 6 inches in diameter, the other about 4 inches in diameter. Wrap in plastic and refrigerate at least 1 hour (or up to 2 days), or freeze for up to 1 month.

Bring a large pot of salted water to a boil. Add the kale and blanch, stirring occasionally, until the leaves are wilted, 3 to 4 minutes. Work in batches, moving the blanched kale to a colander to drain as you work. Let cool, then squeeze dry. Get out as much moisture as you can, then chop roughly; squeeze dry again. You should have 2 generous cups of tightly packed, cooked kale. Set aside.

Heat the olive oil in a large sauté pan or skillet over medium heat. Add the pancetta and cook, stirring often, until the fat is rendered and the pancetta is golden brown and crisp, about 8 minutes. Use a slotted spoon to remove the pancetta to a paper towel–lined plate. Leave the fat in the pan.

Add the garlic to the pan and stir until fragrant, about 1 minute. Add the onions and cook until softened, stirring occasionally, about 6 minutes. Set aside.

In a large bowl, mix together the 2 eggs and ricotta. Stir in the remaining 3 ounces Parmesan, oregano, and ½ teaspoon black pepper. Add the cooked kale, sautéed pancetta, cooked onions, pine nuts, and red pepper (if using). Mix well to break up the packed kale and distribute the ingredients evenly. Season with a big pinch of salt.

On a lightly floured surface, use a lightly floured rolling pin to roll the larger dough disc to a 12-inch round, a generous ⅛ inch thick. Carefully fold in half, slide onto the rolling pin, and transfer to a 9-inch standard pie pan. Unfold, easing the dough gently into the pan and letting the excess drape over the sides; do not stretch the dough. Spoon in the kale mixture, spreading it evenly. Brush egg wash along the rim.

On a freshly floured surface, use a freshly floured rolling pin to roll the second dough disc to about an 11-inch round, a generous ⅛ inch thick. Carefully fold the dough in half, slide onto the rolling pin, and transfer to the top of the pie. Trim the edges, leaving a ½-inch overhang, then fold under and press together. Flute or crimp decoratively. Refrigerate until chilled, about 20 minutes.

Meanwhile, place an oven rack in the center position. Preheat the oven to 375°F.

Brush the top of the chilled pie lightly with egg glaze. Use a sharp knife to pierce 6 or 8 steam vents decoratively into the crust. Transfer to a rimmed baking sheet and bake until golden brown, about 1 hour.

Let rest on a wire rack at least 20 minutes before slicing. Serve warm or at room temperature.

Asiago Mac-n-Cheese Pie with Potato Crust

This "pie" is dense with pasta, creamy Asiago cheese, and prosciutto. I call it a pie, but it's really a variation on timballo di maccheroni, *a traditional drum-shaped baked pasta dish from Naples and the surrounding Campania region of Italy. Some years ago, the preparation of a* timballo di maccheroni *was featured in a movie called* Big Night. *It made a big impression on audiences, myself included. Suddenly it came to the attention of Americans. Since then I've made many variations of this dish—but the more I make it, the more it becomes (at least in my mind) another great take on good ole mac and cheese.*

MAKES 6 TO 8 SERVINGS

1 pound russet potatoes, peeled and cut into 2-inch chunks

½ teaspoon kosher salt, plus more as needed

1 tablespoon unsalted butter

½ teaspoon truffle oil (optional)

2 green onions (white, light green, and some dark green parts), minced

Freshly cracked black pepper

1 teaspoon vegetable oil

2 cups whole milk

3 cups loosely packed, grated Asiago cheese

¼ teaspoon red pepper flakes

⅛ teaspoon freshly grated nutmeg

3 large eggs, lightly beaten

1 pound uncooked tube pasta (such as penne, rigatoni, or macaroni)

12 fresh sage leaves, cut crosswise into very thin strips

2 ounces thinly sliced prosciutto, cut into ½-inch ribbons

¼ cup fresh breadcrumbs, made from crustless white sandwich bread

¼ cup grated Parmesan cheese, plus more for passing

Place the potatoes and ½ teaspoon salt in a large saucepan with enough water to cover by about 1 inch. Bring to a boil, reduce to simmer, cover, and cook until the potatoes fall apart when poked with a fork, about 20 minutes. Strain and return to the hot, dry saucepan. Reduce the heat to low and cook, uncovered, shaking the pan often to evaporate as much water from the potatoes as you can, about 4 minutes. Let the potatoes cool somewhat, then push them through a ricer into a medium bowl (or use a masher or fork). Stir in the butter, truffle oil, if using, and green onions. Season to taste with salt and pepper. Let cool somewhat.

Place an oven rack in the center position. Preheat the oven to 375°F.

Grease the bottom and sides of a 9 or 10-inch springform pan with vegetable oil. Using your fingers, press the potato mixture evenly across the bottom. Bake until lightly browned on the edges, about 25 minutes. Cool on a rack.

Bring the milk to a boil in a medium saucepan over medium heat, stirring occasionally. Remove and stir in the Asiago, red pepper, and nutmeg. Let cool slightly, then briskly whisk in the eggs. Season with a pinch more each of salt and pepper. Cook the pasta according to the package directions until al dente. Drain well.

Fold the pasta, Asiago mixture, and sage together in a large bowl. Add the prosciutto ribbons in several stages to keep them from clumping, stirring after each addition until well combined. Spread three-fourths of the mixture evenly over the potato crust, pressing down lightly to fill any large gaps.

❧ WINE PAIRING

Soave Classico, preferably Soave Superioré.

Made mostly from the Garganega grape variety, Soave Superioré wines smell and taste of yellow apple, pear, and tangerine, with hints of orange blossom and almonds. Weightier than basic Soave, this wine stands up to the pasta's rich sauce, and I like the wine's nuttiness with cheese. Both the wine and the Asiago cheese come from Italy's Veneto region. Recommended producers: Pieropan, Gini, Inama.

Heap the remaining pasta mixture decoratively on top, allowing space for the exposed pasta tips to get nicely brown. Top with the breadcrumbs and Parmesan. Bake on a rimmed baking sheet until well browned, 40 to 45 minutes.

Let cool on a rack about 15 minutes. Run a table knife around the edge and remove the springform mold. Slice into wedges and serve warm, passing additional Parmesan at the table.

Duck Ragu Pasticcio

The heart of this recipe is the rich, flavorful duck ragu. I was inspired by chef and author Lidia Bastianich to begin the layering of deep flavors into the braised duck through the use of soffritto*. This slow-cooked onion and tomato building block is common in Mediterranean cooking. (I say "inspired," because I've simplified the process; a true* soffritto *can take hours to prepare.) I then layered the ragu with mustard greens into a* pasticcio—*a generic term in Italian kitchens for ingredients layered in a pie. Such pies often contain pasta. In this case I've used macaroni—because macaroni is fun.*

MAKES 6 TO 8 SERVINGS

Basic Pie Pastry (page 16)*

1 ounce dried mushrooms (such as porcini)

1½ cups warm water

3½ pounds fresh or frozen and thawed duck legs with thighs attached, rinsed and patted dried with paper towels

Kosher salt and freshly cracked black pepper

2 tablespoon olive oil

1 medium onion, coarsely chopped

2 ounces fresh cremini mushrooms, coarsely chopped

2 tablespoons tomato paste

1 cup Marsala wine

2 cups chicken broth

1 bay leaf

2 teaspoons minced fresh thyme leaves

6 whole cloves

¼ teaspoon red pepper flakes

¼ teaspoon anise seeds

4 ounces uncooked elbow macaroni, or similar pasta

2 tablespoons unsalted butter

1 tablespoon flour, plus more for rolling

¾ cup whole milk

4 ounces fontina cheese, grated

4 cups chopped, lightly packed mustard greens

3 ounces low-moisture mozzarella cheese, thinly sliced

1 egg yolk lightly beaten with 1 teaspoon water, for egg wash

* Other choices: Cream Cheese Crust (page 17), Extra-Rich Short Pastry (page 19), and Gluten-Free Pie Pastry (page 20).

Prepare the pastry recipe and shape the dough into 2 discs ¾ inch thick—one about 6 inches in diameter, the other about 4 inches in diameter. Wrap in plastic and refrigerate at least 1 hour (or up to 2 days), or freeze for up to 1 month.

In a bowl, cover the dried mushrooms with the warm water and let stand at least 20 minutes until softened. Strain the liquid through a paper towel–lined sieve into a clean bowl; set aside. Rinse the rehydrated mushrooms well, then coarsely chop; set aside.

Remove most of the skin and fat from the duck thighs, but leave the drumstick skin attached. Season with salt and pepper. Heat 2 tablespoons olive oil in a large, heavy-bottomed Dutch oven over medium-high heat until nearly smoking. Sear the duck in batches until lightly browned on all sides, about 6 minutes. Transfer to a paper towel–lined plate.

Reduce the heat to medium. Add the onion and cook, stirring often, until just softened, about 5 minutes. Add the fresh mushrooms and a pinch each of salt and pepper. Cook, stirring often, until the mushrooms give off their liquid, about 5 minutes. Add the rehydrated mushrooms and tomato paste. Cook, stirring often, until the tomato paste begins to caramelize and separate from the oil, about 6 more minutes. Pour in the Marsala, scraping the bottom to loosen any browned bits. Add the chicken broth, mushroom-soaking liquid, bay leaf, thyme, cloves, red pepper, and anise seeds. Raise the heat and bring to a boil, then reduce to a simmer. Add the duck to the pot along with any accumulated juices.

❧ WINE PAIRING

Italian Barbera from the Piedmonte region, preferably d'Alba.

With soft, sweet red fruit flavors and a touch of spice and wood smoke, Barbera has medium body and low tannins that make for a good pairing with duck. Its high acidity also makes it a perfect partner for many tomato-based sauces. I especially like Barbera with recipes that contain mushrooms. Recommended producers: Vietti, Pico Maccario, Michele Chiarlo.

Cover and gently simmer 30 minutes. Turn the duck pieces over, partially cover with the lid slightly ajar, and simmer another 30 minutes. Turn the duck again, remove the lid, and simmer for a final 30 minutes, until the meat is very tender and the sauce has thickened (1½ hours total simmering time).

Transfer the duck to a cutting board until cool enough to handle. Strain the sauce into a medium bowl, pressing the solids to extract maximum flavor. Wipe the pot with a paper towel and pour the sauce back in; you should have about 3½ cups. Reduce to 2 cups over medium heat, about 20 minutes. Skim off any fat or scum. Adjust the seasoning as needed with salt and pepper. Set aside to cool.

When the duck is cool enough to handle, remove and discard the skin and fat. Pull the meat from the bones and use 2 forks to shred it. Return to the pot with the sauce and cook over medium heat, uncovered, stirring occasionally, until you have a thick, meaty sauce, at least 20 minutes. Add a good grind of black pepper and let cool. (The ragu may be made up to 2 days ahead and refrigerated, covered. Let it come to room temperature before continuing.)

In a large pot of salted water, cook the pasta to al dente stage according to the package instructions, about 6 minutes. While it cooks, melt the butter in a medium saucepan over medium heat. Stir in 1 tablespoon flour until a paste forms. Gradually pour in ¼ cup milk, whisking until a thick paste begins to be released from the bottom. Reduce the heat, add the remaining ½ cup milk, and cook until thickened, whisking often, about 5 minutes. Remove from the heat. Stir in the fontina until the sauce is smooth and the cheese is melted. Season to taste with salt and pepper.

Drain the pasta in a colander, shaking off excess moisture. Pour into the cheese sauce, stirring to combine. Set aside.

On a lightly floured surface, use a lightly floured rolling pin to roll the larger dough square to about 13 x 13 inches, a generous ⅛ inch thick. Carefully fold in half, slide onto the rolling pin, and transfer to an 8 x 8 x 2-inch-deep baking dish. Unfold, easing the dough gently into the dish; do not stretch. Let the excess overhang evenly. Spoon in the cooled duck mixture, spreading it evenly; it should come up a bit more than halfway. Spread mustard greens on top, followed by the macaroni mixture. Top with mozzarella slices. Use your hands to compact the filling level with the top of the dish. Brush egg wash along the overhanging pastry edge.

On a freshly floured surface, use a freshly floured rolling pin to roll the second dough square to about 9 x 9 inches. Fold in half, slide onto the rolling pin, and transfer to the top of the pie. Trim, leaving a ½-inch overhang. Fold under and press the edges together; flute or crimp decoratively. Refrigerate until chilled, at least 30 minutes.

Place an oven rack in the center position. Preheat the oven to 425°F.

Brush the chilled dough top with egg wash and sprinkle with salt. Use a knife to pierce a few steam vents decoratively in the crust. Transfer to a rimmed baking sheet, set in the oven, and immediately lower the heat to 375°F. Bake until golden brown, about 1 hour. Allow to cool on a rack at least 20 minutes. Slice and serve warm.

NOTE

You can make this pie in any shape of baking dish, casserole, or pie pan that's about 2 quarts in size. Roll and shape the dough accordingly.

Porchetta Pot Pies with Rosemary and Juniper

Way before American barbecue, there was the Italian pampered pig in a pit. Porchetta *is a whole roasted sucking pig—a common feature at outdoor Tuscan festivals and holidays. It's typically stuffed with armloads of herbs and fistfuls of garlic. In its full-size form it's a marvel of sweet pork and aromatics. But chances are you can't get a whole pig into your refrigerator, let alone into a pie. So try this version instead.*

MAKES 6

Basic Pie Pastry (page 16)*

2½ to 3-pound boneless pork shoulder roast

5 tablespoons minced garlic, divided

3 tablespoon juniper berries, divided

2 teaspoons whole black peppercorns

4 teaspoons fennel seeds, divided

1½ teaspoons kosher salt, divided, plus more as needed

1 tablespoon capers, rinsed and chopped

1 tablespoon grated lemon zest

3 teaspoons minced fresh rosemary, divided

5 tablespoons olive oil, divided

1 carrot, peeled and cut into ¼-inch dice (about 1 cup)

1 stalk celery, cut into ¼-inch dice (about 1 cup)

½ large onion, cut into ¼-inch dice (about 1 cup)

freshly cracked black pepper

3 cups dry white wine, divided

⅓ cup all-purpose flour, plus more for rolling

3 cups chicken broth

1 bay leaf

2 cups fresh blanched or frozen peas

¼ cup coarsely chopped fresh flat-leaf parsley

1 large egg yolk lightly beaten with 1 teaspoon water, for egg wash

* Other choices: Cream Cheese Crust (page 17), Extra-Rich Short Pastry (page 19), and Gluten-Free Pie Pastry (page 20).

Prepare the pastry dough and shape into 2 discs about 5 inches in diameter and ¾ inch thick. Wrap in plastic and refrigerate at least 1 hour (or up to 2 days), or freeze for up to 1 month.

Trim off all but about ¼ inch thick of the roast's exterior fat. Using whatever method you prefer, tie the roast into a tight, uniform shape.

Use a mortar and pestle to lightly grind together 2 tablespoons minced garlic, 2 tablespoons juniper berries, peppercorns, fennel seeds, and 1 teaspoon salt. Mix in a bowl with the capers, lemon zest, 2 teaspoons rosemary, and as much as 2 tablespoons olive oil to form a thick, pastelike consistency. Rub the mixture all over the meat, then cover the roast tightly with plastic wrap. Refrigerate at least 24 hours, or up to 5 days.

Unwrap the roast and let it come to room temperature, about 1 hour. Place an oven rack in the center position and preheat the oven to 350°F.

In a large, heavy-bottomed skillet, heat 2 tablespoons olive oil over high heat until shimmering. Add the roast—it should sizzle. Brown on all sides, 3 to 4 minutes per side. Transfer the skillet to the hot oven. Check after 1 hour; the roast should be starting to brown. Turn it over and cook 2 more hours. Use an instant-read thermometer to check the interior temperature; your goal is 165°F. It may need 15 to 20 minutes more.

Once the roast has reached the desired temperature, remove it from the oven and let it cool completely, loosely covered with foil. Set aside 2 tablespoons of the pan drippings.

❧ WINE PAIRING

Pinot Noir, preferably from Oregon's Willamette Valley.

With its bright cherry flavors, ample acidity, and low tannins, Pinot Noir is a good partner with pork. Its tartness picks up on the capers and lemon in the pork's crust, and there's a mirroring of spiciness in the food and the wine. Extremely food-friendly and very popular, Pinot Noir is every cook's best friend. Recommended producers: Ken Wright, Bergström, Torii Mor.

(The roast may be made ahead to this point and kept in the refrigerator, covered, for up to 2 days.)

Remove the string from the roast. Coarsely chop the cooled meat into bite-size chunks. Set aside.

In a large, heavy-bottomed Dutch oven, heat the reserved 2 tablespoons pan drippings and remaining 1 tablespoon olive oil over medium-high heat. Add the carrot, celery, onion, remaining 3 tablespoons garlic, and remaining teaspoon rosemary. Stir to coat; season lightly with salt and pepper. Cook, stirring often, until just beginning to color, about 8 minutes. Reduce the heat to medium and add 1 cup wine. Cook, stirring occasionally, until the wine has evaporated. Add the remaining 2 cups wine and cook, stirring occasionally, until reduced by half, about 8 minutes.

Use a mortar and pestle to crack the remaining 1 tablespoon juniper berries into rough pieces. In a small bowl, whisk the ⅓ cup flour, cracked juniper berries, remaining 1 teaspoon fennel seeds, and ¾ cup broth to form a uniform slurry; stir into the pot. Add the remaining broth, shredded pork, bay leaf, and ½ teaspoon salt and bring to a boil. Reduce to low heat and simmer, partially covered, until the pork is very tender and falling apart, about 1 hour; stir occasionally with a wooden spoon to break the meat up. Turn off the heat off and remove the bay leaf. Stir in the peas and parsley and let cool to room temperature. (The *porchetta* filling can be made up to 2 days ahead and refrigerated, covered; bring to room temperature before continuing.)

Place the oven rack in the center position and preheat the oven to 375°F. On a lightly floured surface, use a lightly floured rolling pin to roll 1 chilled dough disc to a 12 or 13-inch round, a generous ⅛ inch thick. Cut out 3 dough circles about ½ inch larger all around than the ovenproof bowls or ramekins, using a saucer as a template. Repeat with the other dough disc.

Place six 1½ to 2-cup ovenproof bowls or ramekins on a rimmed baking sheet. Divide the *porchetta* filling evenly among them, filling to the top; smooth with the back of the spoon. Brush the rims with egg wash and lay a dough round over each bowl, letting it overhang evenly. Press to seal the edges. Brush with egg wash, make 3 or 4 decorative slits in each top, and sprinkle with salt. Bake until the crust is golden brown and the filling is bubbling, about 50 minutes.

Allow to cool slightly on a wire rack before serving.

"Low-Impact" Rabbit Pie with Creamy Mustard and Thyme

Rabbit is a fairly rare meat option in most of North America, but it wasn't always like that. During World War II, home-bred rabbits were a patriotic way to deal with the red meat shortage. Once again there are altruistic reasons to consider rabbit as a food source. The environmental impact of raising rabbits is low compared to that of larger animals. The time from conception to maturity is about three months, so they require fewer resources than most animals. The meat from a young rabbit is white and tender. It has a mild flavor and tastes a lot like chicken. You like chicken, don't you?

MAKES 6 TO 8 SERVINGS

Basic Pie Pastry (page 16)*

1 rabbit, skinned and cleaned (about 3 pounds after butchering)

Kosher salt and freshly cracked black pepper

2 thyme sprigs

½ teaspoon whole black peppercorns

5 whole cloves

2 bay leaves

2 tablespoons olive oil

1 cup peeled and coarsely chopped turnips

1 cup peeled and coarsely chopped carrots

1 cup coarsely chopped leeks

¼ cup (½ stick) unsalted butter

⅓ cup all-purpose flour, plus more for rolling

½ cup dry white wine

2 tablespoons grainy English mustard

½ cup sour cream

1 tablespoon minced fresh thyme leaves

1 large egg yolk lightly beaten with 1 teaspoon water, for egg wash

* Other choices: Cream Cheese Crust (page 17), Extra-Rich Short Pastry (page 19), and Gluten-Free Pie Pastry (page 20).

Prepare the pastry dough and shape into 2 discs ¾ inch thick—one about 6 inches in diameter, the other about 4 inches in diameter. Wrap in plastic and refrigerate at least 1 hour (or up to 2 days), or freeze for up to 1 month.

At least 1 hour and up to 3 days ahead, season all sides of the rabbit generously with salt and pepper. Cover tightly in plastic wrap and refrigerate.

Place the thyme sprigs, peppercorns, cloves, and bay leaves on a double layer of cheesecloth. Tie securely to create a bouquet garni. Set aside.

Add the olive oil to a large Dutch oven over medium-high heat. Stir in the turnips, carrots, and leeks and season with a pinch each of salt and pepper. Sauté, stirring often, until the vegetables begin to brown, about 12 minutes. Turn off the heat and use a slotted spoon to transfer the vegetables to a large bowl. Set aside.

Unwrap the rabbit and place in the same Dutch oven, pouring in enough water to barely cover. Turn the heat to high. Add the bouquet garni and bring to a boil, then lower the heat and simmer, covered, until the meat is falling from the bone, about 1½ hours or more. (A wild rabbit will take a lot longer to cook than a domesticated one.) Transfer to a cutting board, leaving the cooking liquid in the pot. Once it's cool enough to handle, pull the meat from the bones, then coarsely chop into bite-size pieces. Place in the bowl with the vegetables.

Remove the bouquet garni from the cooking liquid and set the heat to medium. Cook another 20 to 30 minutes to reduce, skimming the surface often.

Meanwhile, melt the butter in a medium heavy-bottomed saucepan over medium heat. Once the foam subsides, reduce the heat and whisk in ⅓ cup flour until a thick paste forms. Slowly whisk in 1½ cups of reduced cooking liquid, whisking until it begins to thicken and bubble, about 3 minutes. Add the wine, reduce the heat, and simmer 3 more minutes, whisking occasionally. Whisk in the mustard, sour cream, minced thyme, ¼ teaspoon black pepper, and a pinch of salt, if needed. Add to the vegetables and rabbit, mixing well. Let come to room temperature. (The filling can be made up to 2 days ahead and refrigerated, covered. Let it return to room temperature before continuing.)

On a lightly floured surface, use a lightly floured rolling pin to roll out the larger dough disc to a 12 or 13-inch round, a generous ⅛ inch thick. Carefully fold in half, slide onto the rolling pin, and transfer to a 9 or 10-inch pie pan. Unfold, easing the dough gently into the pan and letting the excess overhang evenly; do not stretch the dough. Spoon in the cooled filling, spreading it evenly. Brush egg wash along the rim of the shell.

🍃 WINE PAIRING

Pinot Gris, preferably from Oregon's Willamette Valley.

Because the wine's subtle flavors of lemon, melon, and orange blossom could easily get lost, I like Pinot Gris when paired with simple dishes such as this pie, with its satisfying stew-like filling. There is, however, enough weight and minerality in the wine to complement the slightly gamey flavor of rabbit. Recommended producers: Willakenzie, Chehalem, King Estate.

On a freshly floured surface, use a freshly floured rolling pin to roll the second dough disc to at least an 11-inch round. Carefully fold in half, slide onto the rolling pin, and transfer to the pie top. Trim, leaving a ½-inch overhang, then fold under and press the edges together; flute or crimp decoratively. If you wish, decorate the top. Roll together dough scraps to a generous ⅛-inch thickness and make cutouts in the shape of a running hare. Adhere to the crust with egg wash. Refrigerate until chilled, about 20 minutes.

Place an oven rack in the center position. Preheat the oven to 425°F.

Brush the chilled top crust lightly with egg wash and sprinkle with salt. Use the point of a sharp knife to pierce a few steam vents decoratively in the top. Transfer to a rimmed baking sheet, place in the oven, and immediately lower the temperature to 375°F. Bake until golden brown, about 1 hour. Cool on a rack at least 20 minutes before slicing to serve warm.

Friday Fish Pie

I didn't grow up eating fish pie, but I've grown to love this classic British comfort food. On certain wintry days there is nothing more sublime than the creamy sauce and seafood combination in this all-in-one pie meal. It can be made with just about any fish you can imagine, but I think a background of something firm-fleshed and white is the place to start. I often add salmon for the splash of color it brings to this decidedly beige pie. Some sort of smoked fish is also essential. But the shrimp in this version could easily be replaced by mussels or scallops. Whatever combination you choose, just don't forget the crowd-pleasing crust of fluffy mashed potatoes.

MAKES 6

3 pounds russet potatoes, peeled and cut into 2-inch chunks

1½ teaspoons kosher salt, divided, plus more as needed

½ cup (1 stick) unsalted butter, divided

2 tablespoons milk

White pepper

2 leeks, trimmed, halved lengthwise, and coarsely chopped

1 fennel bulb, halved, cored, and coarsely chopped

3 cups fish broth or clam juice

½ cup dry white wine

1 pound firm-fleshed fish fillet, cut into 1½-inch chunks (choose 1 kind or mix it up)

½ cup all-purpose flour

1 cup heavy cream

¼ cup coarsely chopped fresh flat-leaf parsley

2 anchovy fillets, finely chopped (optional)

1 pound smoked fish (such as trout, whitefish, or kippered herring), broken into 1½-inch pieces

1 pound uncooked, shelled, and deveined small shrimp

Place an oven rack in the center position. Preheat the oven to 400°F.

Place the potatoes and 1 teaspoon salt in a large saucepan with just enough water to cover by about 1 inch. Bring to a boil, then reduce to a simmer, cover, and cook until the potatoes fall apart when poked with a fork, about 20 minutes. Strain and return half the potatoes to the hot, dry pan. Turn the heat to low and cook, uncovered, shaking the pan often to evaporate as much water from the potatoes as you can, about 4 minutes. Transfer to a large bowl. Repeat with the remaining potatoes. When the potatoes have cooled somewhat, push them through a ricer into a medium bowl and beat in 2 tablespoons butter and milk until creamy and fluffy. (Alternatively, you can use a masher or fork.) Season lightly with salt and white pepper. Set aside.

Melt 2 tablespoons butter in a large saucepan over medium heat. Add the leeks and fennel, stirring to coat. Cook, stirring often, until well softened and beginning to color, about 8 minutes. Add the fish broth or clam juice, wine, ½ teaspoon salt, and a pinch of white pepper. Bring to a boil, then reduce to a simmer. Add the raw fish chunks, cover, and simmer until not quite cooked through, about 3 minutes depending on your fish. Gently transfer the fish pieces to a plate, using a slotted spoon, leaving the vegetables in the broth. Raise the heat and bring to a boil. Remove and set aside for at least 15 minutes before continuing.

Melt the remaining 4 tablespoons butter in a large saucepan over medium heat. Sprinkle in the flour and whisk continuously for about 1 minute. Gradually pour in the reserved broth through a strainer, whisking as you work. Discard the vegetable solids. Cook, whisking often, until the sauce thickens and is quite smooth, about 5 minutes. Remove from the heat and stir in the cream, parsley, and anchovies (if using). Adjust the seasoning with more salt and white pepper, if needed. Remove any skin or unappealing bits from the smoked fish and add the pieces to the sauce along with the poached fish chunks and raw shrimp; fold gently to combine.

❧ WINE PAIRING

California Sauvignon Blanc, preferably lightly oaked.

This style of Sauvignon Blanc, with its grassy, citrus, ripe melon, tropical fruit, and vanilla flavors, is usually richer than the well-known New Zealand examples. Its crisp acidity, however, will cut through the fish pie's dense filling, and the slight smokiness from the oak will pick up on the smoked fish. This is truly a "can't miss" wine with almost any seafood. Recommended producers: Peter Michael, Clark-Claudon, Ferrari-Carano.

Divide the fish mixture among six 2-cup ramekins or ovenproof bowls, leaving about ¾ inch space on top; you may have extra fish mixture. Dollop mashed potatoes on top to cover the surface of each pie. Place at least 2 inches apart on a parchment-lined rimmed baking sheet (the sauce will probably bubble over). Bake until the potato crust is browned in places, about 40 minutes. Serve hot.

NOTE

Alternatively, you can make this recipe as a single pie in a shallow 1½ to 2-quart baking dish or casserole; give it 5 to 10 additional minutes in the oven.

Caramelized Fennel and Onion Pissaladière

This completely delicious tart from the south of France takes its name from the odd-sounding (to English-speakers) French word for puréed anchovies, pissalat. But don't let that stop you from giving this recipe a try. Traditionally this tart is made with lots of onions, anchovies, and black olives. My version adds sweetly caramelized fennel and a kick of anise-flavored Pernod. You can leave out the anchovies if you like, but why would you give up the opportunity to say "pissalat"?

MAKES 6 SERVINGS

4 tablespoons olive oil, plus more for the baking sheet

5 medium onions (about 2 pounds), very thinly sliced

2 fennel bulbs (about 1 pound), cored and very thinly sliced

½ teaspoon kosher salt, plus more as needed

2 tablespoons minced fresh thyme leaves, divided

2 tablespoons water, plus more as needed

2 ounces Pernod or other anise-flavored liqueur

Freshly cracked black pepper

1 pound Easy Flatbread Dough (page 18) or purchased pizza dough

3 (2-ounce) tins anchovy fillets, drained (optional)

Pitted jarred kalamata or black olives

Heat the olive oil in a large, lidded saucepan or Dutch oven over medium heat. Add the sliced onions, fennel, ½ teaspoon salt, and 1 tablespoon thyme, stirring to coat well. Cook, stirring often, until the vegetables begin to caramelize slightly, about 12 minutes. Add 2 tablespoons water, cover, and reduce to very low heat. Cook, stirring occasionally and adding a touch of water once or twice if needed, until the vegetables are lightly golden and very soft, about 40 minutes. Deglaze with Pernod, scraping up any browned bits. If the mixture is quite wet, remove the lid and increase the heat to cook another minute or so. Season with pepper. Set aside to cool somewhat.

Place a pizza stone on the lowest rack of a cold oven and turn the oven to its highest temperature, about 500°F. You want the stone very hot, so leave ample time for it to heat through. (I like the pizza stone from King Arthur Flour, which measures ½ x 14½ x 16½ inches.)

Lightly oil a 10 x 15-inch rimmed baking sheet or the equivalent. Roll dough to fit and transfer to the baking sheet. Using your fingertips, press the dough into the corners and along the edges to completely cover. Let rest about 5 minutes. If the dough retracts, press it out and let it rest again. Repeat until it no longer retracts. Spread the fennel mixture evenly on top. Lay the anchovies, if using, in a diagonal lattice pattern. Arrange olives in each diamond.

Place the baking sheet directly on the hot pizza stone. Bake until the edges are nicely browned, 18 to 20 minutes depending on your oven's temperature. Remove and sprinkle with the remaining thyme. Cut into 12 squares to serve hot, warm, or at room temperature.

Pizza Rustica (Italian Easter Pie)

This is not a pizza. It's an unusual pie with a pedigree dating back to medieval times. It has a slightly sweet crust and a savory filling, like many of the stuffed pastries of that time. In Italy, this "ham-stuffed" pie is traditionally eaten as part of the Easter celebration. Sometimes you see it with a yeasty crust, but a slightly sweet wrapper—known as pasta frolla—*is more traditional. If you prefer a savory crust, leave out the sugar.*

I like to make my pie in a straight-sided pan or ring mold. A springform pan works nicely, because it lets me remove the pie for a beautiful presentation.

MAKES 6 TO 8 SERVINGS

6 whole eggs, divided

2 egg yolks

3½ cups all-purpose flour, plus more for rolling

¼ cup sugar (optional)

1 teaspoon kosher salt, divided

1 cup (2 sticks) very cold European-style (high-fat) unsalted butter, cut into ½-inch dice

15 ounces ricotta, well-drained

6 ounces thickly sliced prosciutto, cut into ¼-inch dice

6 ounces thickly sliced soppressata, cut into ¼-inch dice

6 ounces thickly sliced pepperoni, cut into ¼-inch dice

6 ounces thickly sliced low-moisture mozzarella cheese, cut into ¼-inch dice

4 ounces thickly sliced provolone cheese, cut into ¼-inch dice

½ cup grated pecorino Romano cheese (or Parmesan, if you prefer)

2 tablespoons minced fresh flat-leaf parsley

½ teaspoon freshly cracked black pepper

Note: Cooked ham in the same amounts can be substituted for any or all of the Italian meats listed in the ingredients.

In a small bowl, beat 2 whole eggs and 2 egg yolks together until well combined. Set aside.

In the bowl of a food processor, pulse 3½ cups flour, sugar (if using), and ½ teaspoon salt until well combined. Add the butter and process about 6 to 8 seconds, until the mixture is crumbly and coarse, with small chunks of butter visible throughout. Add the egg mixture and process until the dough just comes together and begins to pull away from the sides, about 15 seconds. Shape into 2 discs ¾ inch thick, one about 8 inches in diameter and the other about 5 inches in diameter. Wrap in plastic and refrigerate least 1 hour (or up to 2 days), or freeze for up to 1 month.

Mix the ricotta and remaining 4 whole eggs in a large bowl until completely combined. Stir in the prosciutto, soppressata, pepperoni, mozzarella, provolone, pecorino, parsley, and black pepper. Add the remaining ½ teaspoon salt or not, depending on the salt content of the meats—use your judgment.

On a lightly floured surface, use a lightly floured rolling pin to roll the larger chilled pastry disc into a 13-inch round, a generous ⅛ inch thick. Line a 9-inch pie pan or an 8 x 2-inch-deep, straight-sided ring mold or springform pan with pastry, letting the excess drape over the sides. Lining a straight-sided ring mold or pan can be a bit tedious. Work slowly. You'll need to pinch off or press flat the excess dough from the folds that appear as you work. Repair the inevitable cracks with scraps. The extra work pays off in a beautiful presentation with just the right ratio of dough to filling.

Scrape the filling into the lined pan and smooth with the back of the spoon. It should come to the rim. Moisten the overhanging edge with a little water, using your finger.

Roll the remaining pastry to at least a 9 or 10-inch round, a generous ⅛ inch thick. Cover the pie, pressing all around to seal. Trim neatly or decoratively, as you see fit; save the excess dough for another use. If you're using a pie pan, you can crimp the edge. Refrigerate, covered, until chilled, about 30 minutes. Meanwhile, place an oven rack in the center position and preheat the oven to 400°F.

Use a small, sharp knife to make 4 or 5 small slits as steam vents. Place the pie on a rimmed baking sheet and bake for 50 minutes, until the crust is golden and the filling is cooked through. If using a mold or springform pan, let cool completely before removing the ring. Slice and serve at room temperature.

Shrimp and Grits Pot Pies

I hope you won't think this dish is too spicy, too lemony, or altogether too much. When I sat down to develop the recipe, I'd only eaten shrimp and grits made by a cook who lived in Cairo, Georgia, in the 1980s. Rose was a big woman who used a big hand when it came to everything she loved. That included Tabasco sauce and lemon. Oh, and cheese.

My version of this Southern classic is a pot pie. I've cut down somewhat on the cheese in the grits, but I've left the Tabasco bold and the lemon bright—and I've opted for real lemon instead of the ReaLemon used by Rose.

MAKES 4 SERVINGS

6 cups chicken broth, divided

1 cup white stone-ground grits

¼ cup plus 4 tablespoons grated white Cheddar cheese, as sharp as you like, divided (use the "yeller" Cheddar if you want—Rose would)

3 tablespoons butter, plus more if needed

Kosher salt and white pepper

1½ pounds medium shrimp, peeled and deveined

Juice of 2 lemons

5 or 6 dashes red Tabasco sauce, or more as needed

6 slices bacon

3 cloves garlic, minced

½ cup coarsely chopped green onions (white, light green, and some dark green parts)

½ cup all-purpose flour

2 tablespoons chopped fresh flat-leaf parsley

1 teaspoon grated lemon zest

¼ teaspoon red pepper flakes (optional)

cayenne pepper (optional)

In a medium saucepan over medium heat, bring 3 cups broth to a boil. Whisk in the grits until they begin to boil. Reduce the heat to simmer and cook, stirring often, until the grains are thick and tender, about 10 minutes depending on the grits. Add ¼ cup cheese and 3 tablespoons butter; season with a big pinch each of salt and white pepper. Whisk just until the cheese is melted. Cover and remove from the heat.

In a bowl, toss the shrimp with lemon juice and Tabasco. Set aside to "cook" in the acid.

Place an oven rack in the center position. Preheat the oven to 425°F.

Lay the bacon flat in a large, unheated cast-iron skillet. Turn the burner to medium and cook until crispy, turning often, about 8 minutes. Drain on a paper towel–lined plate. Crumble or chop and set aside.

Pour off all but about 3 tablespoons of the bacon fat. (If you have less than that, add a bit of butter.) Add the garlic and green onions to the skillet, stirring to coat. Sprinkle in the flour and sauté until brown and crumbly, about 1 minute. Slowly pour in 1 cup broth, whisking until smooth. Add the remaining 2 cups broth, whisking until you have a smooth, thick sauce, about 6 minutes. Remove from the heat. Whisk in the shrimp marinade (but not the shrimp), parsley, lemon zest, red pepper, if using, and bacon. Season to taste with salt, pepper, and a bit more Tabasco.

Divide the shrimp among four 1½ to 2-cup ramekins or ovenproof bowls. Spoon in sauce to about ¾ inch from the top; don't overfill. Mound one-fourth of the grits in each ramekin and spread evenly; you may need to gently reheat with a couple teaspoons water to get a spreadable consistency.

Place on a rimmed, parchment-lined baking sheet—they'll probably bubble over. Divide the remaining Cheddar on top, followed by a light dusting of cayenne, if using. Heat until the grits begin to brown and the shrimp are cooked through, about 15 minutes. Serve hot.

❧ WINE PAIRING

California Viognier or Viognier blend.

Wines made from Viognier grapes are intensely aromatic, packed with peach, pear, and white flower fragrances and flavors. The lush, almost viscous texture pairs seamlessly with this dish's creamy grits, and Viognier's subtle sweetness is a natural partner for the succulent shrimp. Highly versatile with food, Viognier also makes a great aperitif. Recommended producers: Tablas Creek, Bonny Doon, Sobon Estate.

Sausage and Red Pepper Polenta Cobbler

In North America, cobblers are typically thought of as sweet, made with the best of the season's fruit. But Old World versions were more likely to be savory. Since cobblers get their name from the cobblestone streets common to villages in Europe, I thought a savory version deserved attention. Mine has sausage and red peppers—classic Italian partners—baked under a cobbled polenta topping.

MAKES 4 SERVINGS

1 tablespoon olive oil

4 or 5 spicy Italian sausages (about 1 pound), removed from their casings

Kosher salt and freshly cracked black pepper

1 medium onion, halved lengthwise and thinly sliced

2 red bell peppers, halved and sliced lengthwise into ¼-inch strips

1¾ cups all-purpose flour, divided

2 cups chicken broth

2 tablespoons tomato paste

3 cups loosely packed baby spinach (about 3 ounces)

½ cup quick-cooking polenta mix or yellow cornmeal

1 teaspoon baking powder

1 teaspoon baking soda

1 cup grated Parmesan cheese

6 tablespoons (¾ stick) chilled, unsalted butter, cut into ½-inch dice

1¼ cups heavy cream, plus 1 tablespoon for brushing

Heat the olive oil in a 12-inch cast-iron or other ovenproof skillet over medium-high heat. Add the sausage and season with a pinch each of salt and pepper. Cook until browned, breaking up with a wooden spoon, about 10 minutes. Using a slotted spoon, remove the sausage from the skillet. Pour off all but about 2 tablespoons fat.

Add the onion to the skillet and cook, stirring occasionally, until somewhat softened, about 5 minutes. Add the pepper strips and cook 5 more minutes, stirring occasionally. Season to taste with salt and pepper.

Meanwhile, in a medium bowl whisk together ¼ cup flour and the tomato paste. Slowly whisk in the chicken broth until well combined; add to the skillet. Stir in the spinach and sausage and cook about 2 minutes, until slightly thickened. Remove from the heat and adjust the seasoning, if needed. (The filling may be prepared several hours ahead to this point; let come to room temperature, then cover and refrigerate.)

Place an oven rack in the center position. Preheat the oven to 375°F.

In a medium bowl, whisk together the remaining 1½ cups flour, polenta, baking powder, baking soda, and ½ teaspoon salt. Using a pastry blender, 2 butter knives, or your fingers, cut or rub in the butter until the mixture resembles coarse crumbs with various-size chunks of butter visible throughout. Add the Parmesan, cutting or rubbing to lightly mix. Stir in 1¼ cups cream until a rough dough forms.

Drop 6 or 8 large mounds of polenta mixture over the sausage mixture, 1 inch apart. Brush the remaining 1 tablespoon cream on top. Bake until the filling is bubbly and the polenta topping is golden brown, about 25 minutes; a knife inserted in the center should come out clean. Bring the skillet to the table and serve warm.

Salmon Loaf en Croûte

Here's my version of an haute cuisine classic from the 1950s, originally a whole sea bass baked in a shell of golden puff pastry. This culinary masterpiece came from the kitchen of Fernand Point, the father of modern French cuisine. His version has the delicate croûte *fancifully styled into the form of a fish. In my slightly more humble incarnation, I've filled the* croûte *with a beautiful salmon loaf. The result is super-delicious and spectacular-looking, but deceptively easy if you use store-bought pastry.*

MAKES 4 SERVINGS

1⅓ pounds boneless, skinless wild Alaskan salmon fillets, coarsely cut into chunks

¼ cup plus 2 tablespoons minced fresh chives, divided, plus more for garnish

2 teaspoons lightly crushed fennel seeds

1 teaspoon grated lemon zest

¾ teaspoon kosher salt, plus more as needed

White pepper cooking spray (optional) flour for rolling

2 (14-ounce) packages frozen all-butter puff pastry, thawed in the refrigerator*

1 cup fresh arugula or baby spinach leaves

2 egg yolks lightly beaten with 2 teaspoons water, for egg wash

2 teaspoons vegetable oil

1 medium shallot, minced

1 cup heavy cream

½ cup clam juice

½ teaspoon Asian fish sauce (optional)

1 Roma tomato, peeled, seeded, and cut into ⅛-inch dice

* Two sheets from a 17.3-ounce package of puff pastry can be stacked, folded, and rolled together as a substitute for each of the 14-ounce package listed above; you'll have pastry left over.

In the bowl of a food processor, pulse the salmon chunks 10 to 12 times until the texture resembles slightly wet, coarsely ground beef. Transfer to a medium bowl and stir in ¼ cup chives, fennel seeds, lemon zest, and a pinch each of salt and white pepper. Divide into 4 equal portions and form into 5 x 2-inch slope-sided loaves, being careful not to work the mixture too much. Cover and refrigerate at least 20 minutes. (The loaves can be made up to 24 hours ahead to this point.)

Lightly spray 2 rimmed baking sheets with cooking spray and line with parchment paper; the spray is optional but will keep the parchment flat when you form the fish. Set aside.

On a lightly floured surface, use a lightly floured rolling pin to roll 1 package puff pastry to about a 10 x 15-inch rectangle, a generous ⅛ inch thick. Cut crosswise and lengthwise to make four 5 x 7½-inch rectangles. Lay 2 rectangles on each prepared baking sheet, spaced well apart.

Center ¼ cup arugula or baby spinach on each piece of pastry, leaving a 1¼-inch border all around. Set a chilled salmon loaf on top. Tuck stray leaves under the salmon loaf so they won't interfere when you seal the dough later.

On a freshly floured surface, use a freshly floured rolling pin to roll the second package of pastry into a 10 x 15-inch rectangle. Cut into four 5 x 7½-inch rectangles. Brush a thin border of egg wash all around a salmon loaf to act as glue. Center a piece of pastry on top. Let the weight of the pastry do the work as you drape it over the salmon and allow it to meet the bottom pastry without too much stretching. Gently press the top smooth and flattened somewhat, forcing the air bubbles out. Press the pastry edges together, using the side of a knife or an offset spatula to assure a tight seal. Repeat with the other loaves.

You now have a couple of options. You can crimp and trim each packet into an oval with a neat ½-inch lip all around, or you can be fanciful and shape each one into a fish by using pastry trimmings to form fins, gills, a mouth, and eyes. Be as creative as you like, using various tools to form scales, but be careful not to cut all the way through. Double-check the seal all around the edges. Refrigerate until chilled, about 20 minutes. Place oven racks in the center and upper positions. Preheat the oven to 425°F. Brush the exposed dough with egg wash, being careful not to let it drip onto the parchment—that could make it hard to remove. Bake for 5 minutes, then reduce the temperature to 375°F and bake until the pastry is puffed and deeply golden, about 15 to 20 minutes more. Rotate the baking sheets halfway through.

While the fish bakes, warm the vegetable oil in a small saucepan over medium-high heat. Add the minced shallot and a small pinch of salt. Cook, stirring occasionally, until the shallot has softened but not yet colored, about 5 minutes. Pour in the cream and clam juice. Bring almost to a boil, then lower to a simmer. Cook until thickened, swirling the pan occasionally, about 15 minutes. Remove from the heat and stir in the fish sauce, if using, tomato, and remaining 2 tablespoons chives. Taste for seasoning, adding a pinch each of salt and white pepper if needed. Move the baking sheets to racks to cool about 5 minutes. Spoon a bit of sauce onto 4 warmed plates and set the salmon loaves *en croûte* on top or next to the sauce. Garnish with more chives. Serve warm.

Corn Pudding Pie with Chiles and Chicken

Drive through the region near Hatch, New Mexico, just before the first frost is expected, and you'll encounter plumes of fragrant smoke billowing from backyards. These aren't smoke signals, but they might as well be. They signal the end of chile season, a time when hand-cranked roasters are working overtime to process the last of the chiles that have made this region famous. It's a beautiful time of year. That's a big part of the culinary romance attached to Hatch chiles, which I fully endorse. But to be fair, Hatch is less a chile variety than it is a chile from a particular area. Whatever the botanical facts may be, chiles from Hatch are exceptional. I like a variety known as Big Jim.

MAKES 6 TO 8 SERVINGS

Extra-Rich Short Pastry (page 19)*

3 tablespoons all-purpose flour, plus more for rolling

6 green onions, trimmed to 8-inch lengths

2 Hatch chiles (or substitute pablanos for more heat or Anaheims for less)

6 ears fresh corn, husked

¼ cup crumbled queso fresco (or substitute well drained ricotta)

2 ounces cream cheese

3 large eggs

3 tablespoons sugar

½ cup whole milk

1 teaspoon salt, plus more as needed

¼ teaspoon freshly cracked black pepper, plus more as needed

4 fried chicken breasts halves, meat removed and shredded with crust attached

* Other choices: Basic Pie Pastry (page 16), Cream Cheese Crust (page 17), and Gluten-Free Pie Pastry (page 20).

Prepare the pastry and shape the dough into 2 discs about 5 inches in diameter and ¾ inch thick. Wrap in plastic and refrigerate at least 1 hour (or up to 2 days), or freeze for up to 1 month.

On a lightly floured surface, use a lightly floured rolling pin to roll 1 chilled dough disc to an 12 or 13-inch round, a generous ⅛ inch thick. Carefully fold in half, slide onto the rolling pin, and transfer to a 9-inch deep-dish pie pan. Unfold, easing the dough gently into the pan and allowing the excess to drape evenly over the sides; do not stretch the dough. Trim, leaving a ½-inch overhang. Fold the overhang under; flute or crimp the edge, if you like. Chill, uncovered, while you make the filling.

Place an oven rack in the center position. Preheat the oven to 375°F.

Heat a large, dry cast-iron or other heavy-bottomed skillet over medium-high heat. Lay the green onions on the bottom in a single layer. Cook undisturbed until they begin to char. Turn with tongs and char the other side. Remove to a cutting board to cool, then chop coarsely.

Repeat the process with the chiles, allowing them to blister and blacken, turning and tamping them flat until all surfaces are well charred. Let the chiles steam in a closed paper bag for about 10 minutes.

Meanwhile, use a knife to cut the kernels from the corn directly into a large bowl. Transfer half of them to a smaller bowl. In the large bowl, whisk the cheeses, eggs, sugar, milk, 3 tablespoons flour, 1 teaspoon salt, and ¼ teaspoon pepper with the corn kernels. Working in batches, roughly purée the mixture in a blender, or use an immersion blender in the bowl. The purée should be well blended but still a bit chunky. With the purée back in the bowl, stir in the reserved corn kernels and chopped green onions.

Remove the chiles from the bag and rub off the blackened skin; it should peel away easily. You needn't remove all the char. Remove the stems and seeds, then chop into ¼-inch dice and stir into the corn mixture. Adjust the seasoning with a pinch more of salt and pepper, if needed.

Scrape the mixture into the dough-lined pie pan and place on a rimmed baking sheet. Bake until the filling is set and golden, about 50 minutes. Let cool on a wire rack about 20 minutes before slicing. Serve warm with shards of chicken on top.

NOTE

If you prefer, you can use baked chicken instead of fried chicken for this recipe.

Irish Breakfast Pie

I love a breakfast that includes eggs with runny yolks, but that's not the only way to go. The eggs in this pie are cooked through.

MAKES 6 TO 8 SERVINGS

Basic Pie Pastry (page 16)

6 slices bacon

1 pound Yukon Gold potatoes

Kosher salt and freshly cracked black pepper

8 large eggs, divided

½ cup heavy cream

1 tablespoon minced fresh flat-leaf parsley

1 egg yolk lightly beaten with 1 teaspoon water, for egg wash

* Other choices: Cream Cheese Crust (page 17), Extra-Rich Short Pastry (page 19), and Gluten-Free Pie Pastry (page 20).

Prepare the pastry and shape into 2 discs ¾-inch thick—one about 6 inches in diameter and the other about 4 inches in diameter. Wrap in plastic and refrigerate at least 1 hour (or up to 2 days), or freeze for up to 1 month.

Place an oven rack in the center position. Preheat the oven to 375°F.

Lay the bacon flat in a large, unheated cast-iron or other heavy-bottomed skillet. Set the heat on medium and cook until crispy, turning often, about 8 minutes. Drain on a paper towel–lined plate, then crumble or roughly chop. Set aside.

Peel and slice the potatoes very thinly. (I like to use a mandoline set to $^{1}/_{10}$ inch, but a sharp knife can also do the job.) Place in a large saucepan and cover with water by about 1 inch. Bring to a full boil, then cook about 2 minutes. The potatoes should be partly cooked but still hold their shape. Drain well and set aside to cool.

On a lightly floured surface, use a lightly floured rolling pin to roll out the larger dough disc to about a 12-inch round, a generous ⅛ inch thick. Carefully fold in half, slide onto the rolling pin, and transfer to a 9-inch pie pan. Unfold, easing the dough gently into the pan without stretching it. Let the excess overhang evenly.

Sprinkle the cooked bacon evenly across the bottom of the pie. Use paper towels to dry the potato slices as you layer them in concentric circles on top of the bacon; add a pinch each of salt and pepper between potato layers. You should get 3 or 4 layers, nearly filling the pan.

In a medium bowl, whisk together 4 eggs, cream, and parsley until frothy. Pour over the potatoes to about ½ inch from top; you may have extra. Carefully crack the remaining 4 eggs on top, gently arranging the yolks so they don't touch and don't break. Season lightly with salt and pepper. Brush egg wash along the rim of the dough.

On a freshly floured surface, use a freshly floured rolling pin to roll the second dough disc to a 10 or 11-inch round. If you like, use a 1½-inch round cutter to press a few holes decoratively around the leaving a 1-inch border; remove the cutouts. Carefully fold the dough in half, slide it onto the rolling pin, and transfer to the top of the pie. It's fine if some of the yolks peek through the holes, but it's not necessary. Take care not to break the yolks. Trim, leaving a ½-inch overhang, then fold under and press the edges together; flute or crimp decoratively. Brush the exposed dough with egg wash.

Place on a rimmed baking sheet and bake until the crust is lightly golden and the eggs and potatoes are cooked though, about 45 minutes. Let cool at least 15 minutes before slicing. Serve warm or at room temperature.

> **NOTE**
>
> The optional cutouts in the top crust are purely decorative. Make them whatever size and shape you like, or omit them and cut steam vents instead. I've even made this pie with good results without a top crust, but be aware that the egg whites will brown in spots during baking.

MAIN COURSE PIES—
VEGETARIAN

English Farmhouse Cheddar Onion Pie

The British love a savory pie—of course, they say "savoury." Some of the most cherished pies in my repertoire find their inspiration in these traditional savouries. Quite a few (not surprisingly) get their comfort from potatoes, baked inside or used as a topping. This recipe is an example of a favorite English countryside pie full of big flavor, starting with the cheese. Cheddar is an English cheese that's been imitated the world over. Great examples can now be found in many countries, but if you can, I suggest you honor the pie's roots by choosing an authentic English Cheddar. Many are still made by traditional methods on the farm.

MAKES 8 SLICES

Basic Pie Pastry (page 16)*

2 medium waxy potatoes (such as red), peeled and cut into ¼-inch dice (about 2 cups)

2 tablespoons unsalted butter

½ large onion, cut into ¼-inch dice (about 1 cup)

2 large eggs

¼ cup heavy cream

¼ cup minced fresh flat-leaf parsley

½ teaspoon English mustard

¼ teaspoon cayenne pepper

¼ teaspoon kosher salt, plus more for shell

¼ teaspoon freshly cracked black pepper

3 cups coarsely grated English farmhouse–style white Cheddar cheese

Flour for rolling

1 large egg yolk lightly beaten with 1 teaspoon water, for egg wash

* Other choices: Cream Cheese Crust (page 17), Extra-Rich Short Pastry (page 19), and Gluten-Free Pie Pastry (page 20).

Prepare the pastry and shape the dough into 2 discs ¾ inch thick—one about 6 inches in diameter and the other about 4 inches in diameter. Wrap in plastic and refrigerate at least 1 hour (or up to 2 days), or freeze for up to 1 month. In a medium bowl, cover the diced potatoes with cool water. Soak 10 minutes to leach out some of the starch. Drain, then transfer to a medium saucepan. Cover with more cool water until just submerged. (Starting with cool water ensures even cooking.) Set over high heat and bring to a boil. Reduce to medium heat and cook until just tender, about 4 minutes. Drain, letting the potatoes cool in the colander.

Melt the butter in a medium skillet over medium heat. Add the diced onion, stirring until well softened, about 8 minutes. Scrape into the colander with the potatoes and let come to room temperature.

In a large bowl, whisk together the eggs, cream, parsley, mustard, cayenne, ¼ teaspoon salt, and pepper. Stir in the cheese and the cooled potatoes and onion. Set aside.

On a lightly floured surface, use a lightly floured rolling pin to roll the larger dough disc to a 12 to 13-inch round, a generous ⅛ inch thick. Carefully fold in half, slide onto the rolling pin, and transfer to a 9-inch pie pan. Unfold, easing gently into the pan; do not stretch the dough. Spoon in the filling, spreading evenly. Brush egg wash along the rim of the shell.

On a freshly floured surface, use a freshly floured rolling pin to roll the second dough disc to about an 11-inch round, a generous ⅛ inch thick. Carefully fold in half, slide onto the rolling pin, and transfer to the top of the pie. Trim, leaving a ½-inch overhang, then fold under and press the edges together; flute or crimp decoratively. Refrigerate until chilled, about 20 minutes.

Meanwhile, place an oven rack in the center position and preheat the oven to 375°F.

Brush the top of the pie lightly with egg wash and sprinkle with kosher salt. Use a sharp knife to pierce 6 or 8 steam vents decoratively into the crust. Transfer to a baking sheet and bake until golden brown, about 50 minutes.

Let cool on a rack at least 30 minutes. Slice into 8 wedges to serve warm or at room temperature.

Shaved Asparagus Galette with Mascarpone and Jarlsberg

I like the idea of changing the way you look at a particular vegetable to make it seem new. Take asparagus, for example. I've eaten it steamed, grilled, baked, broiled, wrapped in prosciutto, and puréed in soups. I've eaten it so many times that it's easy to take for granted. Shaving it into ribbons makes for a striking presentation and a surprisingly delicious and unexpected filling.

MAKES 6 FIRST COURSE OR 4 MAIN COURSE SERVINGS

Cream Cheese Crust (page 17)*

Flour for rolling

1 pound thick or medium asparagus

6 ounces mascarpone cheese, at room temperature

1 large egg, lightly beaten

½ clove garlic, minced

⅛ teaspoon kosher salt, plus more as needed

⅛ teaspoon freshly cracked black pepper, plus more as needed

Pinch of cayenne pepper (optional)

2 ounces Jarlsberg cheese, coarsely grated

1 tablespoon finely grated Parmesan cheese

1 egg yolk lightly beaten with 1 teaspoon water, for egg wash

* Other choices: Basic Pie Pastry (page 16), Extra-Rich Short Pastry (page 19), and Gluten-Free Pie Pastry (page 20).

Prepare the crust dough and shape it into 2 discs about ¾ inch thick, one about 4 inches in diameter and the other about 6 inches. Wrap in plastic and refrigerate at least 1 hour (or up to 2 days), or freeze for up to 1 month.

On a lightly floured surface, use a lightly floured rolling pin to roll the larger dough disc to about a 12 to 13-inch circle, a generous ⅛ inch thick. Transfer it to a parchment-lined baking sheet. Save the other disc for another use.

Place an oven rack in the center position. Preheat the oven to 400°F.

Cut the asparagus tips off in 1½-inch-long pieces; set aside. Working with the stalks, lay 1 at a time on a cutting board aligned with the edge of the countertop. Let the tough end hang over so you can grasp it with your fingertips, leaving the stalk flat on the board. Use a Y-shaped peeler to shave the asparagus into thin ribbons, turning the spear as you work; it's fine if the pieces vary in size. Set the shaved ribbons aside in a medium bowl and discard the tough ends.

In another medium bowl, use a rubber spatula to beat the mascarpone, egg, minced garlic, ⅛ teaspoon each of salt and black pepper, and cayenne, if using, into a smooth and spreadable paste. Scrape the sides often as you work. Spread the mixture evenly over the center of the dough circle, leaving about a 3-inch border all around. Top with grated Jarlsberg, then shaved asparagus, keeping the border intact. Top the galette with the reserved asparagus tips, spreading them around in an attractive manner. Sprinkle with Parmesan.

Fold the dough edge over the filling, pleating as needed to form a neatly rounded package. Don't worry too much about the shape—galettes are freeform pies. Also, don't try to make the dough meet in the middle; you want to leave the filling exposed. Brush the pastry with some egg wash and sprinkle it with salt and pepper.

Bake until the crust is golden and the exposed asparagus tips are beginning to brown, 45 to 50 minutes. Cook on a rack on the baking sheet for about 10 minutes. Transfer the galette to a serving plate. Serve warm or at room temperature.

Fingerling Potato Tart with Radicchio and Gorgonzola

Most of the time, this is a fairly common, uncommonly delicious pizza. I fell in love with it at Pizzeria Mozza in Los Angeles. Italy has a good version, too. Now, thanks to me, it's a tart baked on puff pastry. There's only so much delicious in this world—why not spread it around?

MAKES 6 SLICES

½ pound fingerling or very small Yukon Gold potatoes

2 tablespoons unsalted butter

2 garlic cloves, minced

1 tablespoon minced, plus 2 teaspoons coarsely chopped, fresh rosemary leaves, divided

½ teaspoon kosher salt, plus more as needed

2 tablespoons olive oil, plus more for drizzling (optional)

2 tablespoons water

Flour for rolling

1 (14-ounce) package frozen all-butter puff pastry, thawed in the refrigerator*

½ head radicchio, shredded slaw-style (about 1½ cups)

3 ounces Gorgonzola cheese, crumbled, divided

1 ounce chilled low-moisture mozzarella cheese, cut into ¼-inch dice

Freshly cracked black pepper

* Two sheets from a 17.3-ounce package of puff pastry can be stacked, folded, and rolled together as a substitute for the 14-ounce package listed above; you'll have pastry left over.

Place an oven rack in the center position. Preheat the oven to 400°F.

In a large bowl, toss together the potatoes, butter, garlic, 1 tablespoon minced rosemary, ½ teaspoon salt, 2 tablespoons olive oil, and water. Pour onto a foil-lined baking sheet, cover tightly with more foil, and bake until the potatoes are tender, about 45 minutes depending on the potato size. So check.

Remove the top piece of foil. Using an offset or small, flat spatula, flatten the potatoes to about ½ inch thick, then brush on some of the roasting liquid. Try to space them so they aren't touching. Return to the oven, uncovered, and roast another 15 to 20 minutes, until they just begin to color. Set aside to cool. (You can make the potatoes up to 2 days ahead. Cover and refrigerate once cooled.)

On a lightly floured surface, use a lightly floured rolling pin to roll the puff pastry to about a 10 x 15-inch rectangle, a scant ¼ inch thick. Carefully move it to a parchment-lined baking sheet. Use a ruler and a sharp knife to trim the edges cleanly and lightly score the pastry ¾ inch in from the edges to mark a border; don't cut all the way through. Use a fork to prick the pastry at half-inch intervals inside the border. Refrigerate until chilled, about 20 minutes.

Bake until puffed and barely golden, 8 to 10 minutes. Remove from the oven, pop any large air bubbles, and use a small, flat spatula to flatten the bottom but not the rim. You may need to run a knife along the score line to help with the flattening.

Brush the crust—base and rim—with a little olive oil. Lightly salt. Spread shredded radicchio all over the bottom, inside the rim. Sprinkle on about 2 ounces of Gorgonzola. Break the reserved roasted potatoes into bite-size chunks and lay them evenly on top. Scatter on the remaining Gorgonzola and mozzarella. Sprinkle with remaining 2 teaspoons chopped rosemary and a good grinding of black pepper. Return to the oven and bake until the cheese is melted, bubbly, and starting to brown, about 15 minutes. Start checking at about 12 minutes to make sure the crust doesn't get too brown.

Set the baking sheet on a wire rack to cool for about 10 minutes. Slice the tart into squares and drizzle with a little olive oil, if you wish. Serve warm.

Sweet Potato Tarte Tatin

What a way to celebrate! This sweet potato tarte tatin is a playful nod to the soft, gooey-sweet Thanksgiving side dish of my youth. Taking cues from a classic French dessert made with apples, I give these potatoes a decidedly more elegant, adult spin. Herb-scented maple syrup provides the nostalgic glue, and slices of sweet potatoes are layered on top. I hope you're not afraid of your mandoline, because it's useful for making very thin, very uniform slices. I suggest you invest in a Teflon glove to protect your knuckles. To finish the tart, I use store-bought puff pastry, a valid shortcut in my opinion. I do recommend all-butter brands, such as Dufour. They have a rich flavor and tender, flaky texture that the hydrogenated varieties can't touch.

MAKES 8 SIDE DISH OR 4 MAIN COURSE SERVINGS

Flour for rolling

1 (14-ounce) package frozen all-butter puff pastry, thawed in the refrigerator*

3 tablespoons real maple syrup

1 tablespoon unsalted butter, cut into thin pieces

1 teaspoon fresh thyme leaves

1½ pounds red sweet potatoes or yams, peeled, ends removed, and sliced into ⅛-inch rounds (look for potatoes of fairly even width with few bulges)

Pinch each of kosher salt and freshly cracked black pepper

1 large egg yolk lightly beaten with 1 teaspoon water, for egg wash

* Two sheets from a 17.3-ounce package of puff pastry can be stacked, folded, and rolled together as a substitute for the 14-ounce package listed above; you'll have pastry left over.

Line a baking sheet with parchment paper. On a lightly floured surface, use a lightly floured rolling pin to roll the puff pastry to about a 10 x 15-inch rectangle, a scant ¼ inch thick. Cut into a round with a sharp knife, using a 10 to 11-inch dinner plate as a template. Place on the prepared baking sheet and prick all over with a fork. Refrigerate until chilled, about 20 minutes. Save the trimmings for another use.

Place an oven rack in the center position. Preheat the oven to 400°F.

Pour the maple syrup into an unheated 10-inch cast-iron skillet. Scatter the butter over the syrup, followed by the thyme.

Starting in the center, arrange the sweet potatoes in 2 or 3 layers of overlapping concentric circles on top of the syrup. Season with salt and pepper.

Carefully lay the chilled dough round on top of the sweet potatoes. Tuck in the edges all around the skillet to create a snug fit. Brush the exposed pastry with egg wash and pierce the center with a sharp knife to create a steam vent. Bake until the edges are deep amber and the pastry is puffed and golden, about 30 minutes. Cool on a wire rack for 10 minutes.

Place a serving plate larger than the skillet upside down over the skillet. Using oven mitts or thick kitchen towels in both hands, hold the plate and skillet firmly together in front of you. Quickly invert in a single confident motion, letting the tart fall onto the plate. The plate will now be on the bottom, the skillet upside down on top. Carefully remove the skillet, allowing the tart to settle onto the plate. Be careful—the syrup will be hot. A few potato slices may stick to the skillet; simply remove them with a spatula and place them on the tart.

The end result will be like a traditional tart with crust on the bottom and potatoes on top. Slice into wedges to serve warm.

Roquefort Tart with Sweet Onion Confit

I struggled over whether to call this a quiche or a tart. The most iconic French quiche is from Lorraine, and it's made without cheese. There's cheese in my recipe, and it's from Roquefort—1000 kilometers to the south and miles apart in taste. That's reason enough to think that this is more tart than quiche. Besides, it's baked in a tart pan. So there you go.

MAKES 6 TO 8 SERVINGS

¼ cup olive oil

2 large sweet onions, sliced into ¼-inch rounds, rings separated

1 tablespoon sugar

1½ teaspoons salt, divided

½ cup sherry vinegar

2 tablespoons minced fresh thyme leaves, divided

Extra-Rich Short Pastry (page 19)*

Flour for rolling

4 ounces cream cheese, at room temperature

5 ounces Roquefort cheese, at room temperature

2 tablespoons unsalted butter, melted, at room temperature

3 eggs, lightly beaten

1 cup half and half

¼ teaspoon white pepper

* Other choices: Basic Pie Pastry (page 16), Cream Cheese Crust (page 17), and Gluten-Free Pie Pastry (page 20).

Place an oven rack in the center position. Preheat the oven to 250°F.

Warm the olive oil in a heavy-bottomed, ovenproof saucepan over medium heat. Add the onions, sugar, and 1 teaspoon salt. Cook until softened, stirring often, about 8 minutes. Remove from the heat and stir in the vinegar and 1 tablespoon thyme.

Cut parchment paper to fit inside your saucepan. Press it down over the onions; weigh it with an ovenproof utensil to keep it from curling, if necessary. Cook in the oven until the onions are lightly golden with a jammy consistency, about 2 hours. Begin checking regularly at about 1 hour. Add a touch of water only if needed to keep the pan from drying out; the moisture content of onions varies greatly. (This confit may be made up to 3 days ahead. Bring to room temperature, cover, and chill.)

Prepare the crust dough and shape it into 2 discs about 5 inches in diameter and ¾ inch thick. Wrap in plastic and refrigerate at least 1 hour (or up to 2 days), or freeze for up to 1 month.

On a lightly floured surface, use a lightly floured rolling pin to roll 1 chilled dough disc into an 11 or 12-inch round, a generous ⅛ inch thick. (It can be helpful to roll this dough between sheets of parchment or waxed paper.) Carefully fold in half, slide onto the rolling pin, and transfer to a 9 or 10-inch fluted tart pan. Gently press to line the pan without stretching the dough, using light pressure to push it into the sides. Drape any excess over the sides and run a rolling pin across the top to trim. Patch any tears, or the baked tart could be hard to remove. Generously prick the bottom with a fork. Refrigerate until chilled, about 20 minutes. (Save the other dough disc for another use.) Meanwhile, heat the oven to 400°F.

Line the tart shell with aluminum foil or parchment paper, allowing it to overhang by about 2 inches. Fill with pie weights, copper pennies, rice, or dried beans, spreading them to make sure the edges are supported. Place on a baking sheet and bake until just beginning to color, about 15 minutes. With the tart pan still on the baking sheet, remove the liner and weights. Transfer the tart shell in its pan to a wire rack and let come to room temperature.

Reduce the oven temperature to 300°F.

In a medium bowl, use a fork to mash together the cream cheese, Roquefort, and melted butter to form a rough paste. Add the eggs, half and half, remaining ½ teaspoon salt, white pepper, and remaining 1 tablespoon thyme. Using a hand mixer at medium-low speed, mix until well combined but still slightly lumpy—about the consistency of pancake batter.

Place the tart pan on a rimmed baking sheet. Pour about half the filling into the shell; pour the rest into a small pitcher. Move the tart to the middle rack of the oven, then fill to the rim with filling from the pitcher. Be careful not to overflow, or the tart could be hard to remove. You may not use all the filling.

Bake until puffed and lightly golden brown, about 45 minutes; rotate the pan halfway through. The tart is done when a knife inserted in the center comes out clean. Let cool on a wire rack at least 15 minutes before removing the tart ring. Slice and serve warm or at room temperature, topped with some sweet onion confit.

Grilled Eggplant Flatbreads

I'm mad for Bulgarian sheep's milk feta cheese—though the Greeks will tell you that only Greek-made feta cheese should properly be called feta. In 2002 feta was given "designation of origin" status by the European Union, meaning that only cheeses produced in the traditional way in particular areas of Greece may be called feta. But Bulgarians make and eat a feta-like cheese, too. They call this crumbly, aged white cheese "sirene." Since nobody knows what that is, I continue to call it Bulgarian feta, despite the fact that I know better. All feta is good, however, and would work well in this recipe.

MAKES 8

1½ pounds Easy Flatbread Dough (page 18)

2 teaspoons grated lemon zest

¼ teaspoon paprika

¼ teaspoon ground cinnamon

¼ teaspoon garlic powder

⅛ teaspoon ground cumin

⅛ teaspoon ground coriander

⅛ teaspoon cayenne pepper (optional)

8 Japanese eggplants, stem ends trimmed

Freshly cracked black pepper

Olive oil, as needed

Vegetable oil, as needed

32 pitted green olives, quartered lengthwise

1 pound Bulgarian feta, crumbled

4 teaspoons minced fresh cilantro

High-quality extra-virgin olive oil for drizzling

Prepare the flatbread dough; I prefer milk to water in the dough for this recipe, but either is fine. Once the dough has doubled in size, divide it into 8 flattened balls, then thinly roll each one into a rustic or round shape 7 to 8 inches in diameter. Let rest about 15 minutes, lightly covered.

In a small bowl, mix together the lemon zest, paprika, cinnamon, garlic powder, cumin, coriander, and cayenne, if using. Set aside.

Cut each eggplant lengthwise into 3 or 4 slices approximately ½ inch thick (depending on the size of the eggplant). Lightly brush both sides with olive oil and season with black pepper. I don't think salt is necessary, but you can salt your eggplant if you like.

Heat a grill pan over medium-high heat to the point that you can't hold your hand over it for more than 3 seconds. Working in batches, lay eggplant slices on the grill pan and cook until nicely marked, about 2 minutes per side. I like to weigh them down with a griddle or bacon press (or another pan) to extract some moisture, but that's optional. Transfer slices to a plate as they finish cooking. While hot, sprinkle one side with a generous pinch of the spice blend.

Use a paper towel to wipe a bit of vegetable oil onto a cast-iron or other heavy-bottomed skillet. Set over medium-high heat. Once the skillet is quite hot, cook the flatbreads, one at a time, until puffed and dark brown in spots, 1½ to 2 minutes per side. Set aside.

Heat the broiler to high. Lay 3 or 4 slices of grilled and spiced eggplant on each flatbread, spiced side up. Top with green olives and crumbled feta. Place as many flatbreads on a broiler pan as will comfortably fit and broil until the feta is slightly charred and the flatbread edges are beginning to brown, about 4 minutes depending on the distance from the heat source. Repeat with the remaining flatbreads.

Transfer the flatbreads to a cutting board or serving plate. Garnish with minced cilantro and a drizzle of extra-virgin olive oil. Slice and serve warm.

☙ WINE PAIRING

California Zinfandel, preferably young.

Seen by many as America's own grape, Zinfandel is packed with jammy red and purple fruit flavors and a brambly, peppery bite. The peppery flavors are excellent with the charred eggplant. The soft tannins don't overwhelm this meatless dish yet still stand up to the strong-flavored feta. I look for lighter-style Zins under 15% alcohol. Recommended producers: Turley, Seghesio, Wine Guerrilla.

Baked Egg Shakshuka

Shakshuka is an onomatopoeia in Hebrew and North African languages. Even in English it sounds a lot like what it is—all shook up. It's also perhaps the most popular egg dish in Israel, so popular that it's served at most any time of the day. There are probably about a million different versions. Mine's a bit spicy and may well be the only shakshuka "pie" you've ever seen.

MAKES 4 SERVINGS

Basic Pie Pastry (page 16)*

1 tablespoon plus 1 teaspoon minced fresh thyme leaves, divided

2 tablespoons olive oil

1 large onion, cut into ¼-inch dice (about 2 cups)

1 red bell pepper, cut into ¼-inch dice (about 2 cups)

1 Anaheim chile, ribs and seeds removed, cut into ¼-inch dice (about 1 cup)

Kosher salt and freshly cracked black pepper

2 tablespoons harissa (Tunisian hot chili paste), or to taste

2 cloves garlic, minced

2 teaspoons smoked paprika

½ teaspoon ground cumin

¼ teaspoon red pepper flakes (optional)

3 (14.5-ounce) cans petite-diced tomatoes

½ cup water

Flour for rolling

1 large egg yolk lightly beaten with 1 teaspoon water, for egg wash

4 large eggs

2 tablespoons finely grated Parmesan cheese

1 tablespoon minced fresh flat-leaf parsley

* Other choices: Cream Cheese Crust (page 17), Extra-Rich Short Pastry (page 19), and Gluten-Free Pie Pastry (page 20).

Prepare the pastry recipe, adding 1 tablespoon minced thyme to the flour mixture. Shape into 2 discs about 5 inches in diameter and ¾ inch thick. Wrap in plastic and refrigerate at least 1 hour (or up to 2 days), or freeze for up to 1 month.

In a medium skillet over medium-high heat, heat the oil to shimmering. Add the onion, red bell pepper, Anaheim chile, and a pinch each of salt and pepper. Cook until just softened, about 6 minutes. Add the harissa, garlic, paprika, cumin, and red pepper, if using. Cook until the garlic is soft, stirring frequently, about 2 more minutes. Add the tomatoes with their juice, remaining 1 teaspoon thyme, and water. Reduce to a simmer and cook until thickened, stirring occasionally, about 15 minutes. Remove from the heat and season to taste. Let come to room temperature. (The filling may be made up to 2 days ahead and refrigerated, covered. Let it return to room temperature before continuing.)

Divide each dough disc in half and form each piece into a ball. Flatten slightly with the palm of your hand to a ½-inch thickness. On a lightly floured surface, use a lightly floured rolling pin to roll into rounds about ⅛ inch thick and generously shaped to fit 2-cup ovenproof bowls, ramekins, or gratin dishes. (I find that shallow, slope-sided dishes work best.)

Lay the rolled dough in the dishes, taking care not to stretch it. Let the excess hang or fold evenly over the edge; trim to about a ½-inch overhang. (Much more than that might break off under its own weight during baking.) Refrigerate until chilled, about 20 minutes. Meanwhile, place an oven rack in the center position and preheat the oven to 450°F.

Place the dough-lined dishes on a baking sheet. Spoon a scant 1½ cups tomato mixture into each one. Brush the exposed dough with egg wash and sprinkle with a bit of salt. Bake until the crust is golden and the tomato mixture is bubbly, 12 to 15 minutes.

Carefully remove the baking sheet from the oven and crack an egg into each dish. Season with salt and pepper and a sprinkle of Parmesan and parsley. Bake an additional 8 to 12 minutes, until the whites of the eggs are set and the yolk is cooked to your liking. Serve hot.

NOTE

A convection oven is helpful for achieving baked eggs with whites that are fully cooked and yolks that still run.

Heirloom Tomato Tart

I'm giving top billing to the tomatoes in this tart—which should be an indication that this is the time to seek out the very best tomatoes. These days, too many tomatoes are bred for uniformity of size and color, tricking consumers into believing they have great taste. Look past the obvious and select your tomatoes carefully. Close your eyes and choose with your nose. Backyard beauties are ideal, but good farmers' markets and even most groceries stores have very good heirloom tomatoes in summer.

MAKES 6 TO 8 SERVINGS

Extra-Rich Short Pastry (page 19)

Flour for rolling

1 cup tomato purée (see note)

5 ounces crumbled fresh goat cheese, at room temperature

3 eggs, lightly beaten

½ teaspoon kosher salt

½ teaspoon red Tabasco sauce

Assorted small heirloom tomatoes, as needed

Fresh basil leaves, for garnish

Sea salt, to taste

High-quality extra-virgin olive oil, for drizzling

Aged balsamic vinegar, for drizzling (optional)

* Other choices: Basic Pie Pastry (page 16), Cream Cheese Crust (page 17) and Gluten-Free Pie Pastry (page 20).

Prepare the dough for the crust and shape it into 2 discs about 5 inches in diameter and ¾ inch thick. Wrap in plastic and refrigerate at least 1 hour (or up to 2 days), or freeze for up to 1 month.

On a lightly floured surface, use a lightly floured rolling pin to roll 1 dough disc to an 11 or 12-inch round, a generous ⅛ inch thick. (It can help to roll this dough between sheets of parchment or waxed paper.) Save the other dough disc for another use.

Carefully fold the dough in half, slide it onto the rolling pin, and transfer it to a 9 or 10-inch fluted tart pan. Gently press to line the pan without stretching the dough, using light pressure to push it into the sides. Drape any excess over the sides and run a rolling pin across the top to trim. Patch any tears, or the baked tart may be hard to remove. Generously prick the bottom with a fork. Refrigerate until chilled, about 20 minutes. Save other disc of dough for another use.

Meanwhile, place an oven rack in the center position. Preheat the oven to 400°F.

Line the chilled tart shell with aluminum foil or parchment paper, allowing it to overhang about 2 inches all around. Fill with pie weights, copper pennies, rice, or dried beans, spreading them to support the edges. Place on a baking sheet and bake until just beginning to color, about 15 minutes. With the pan still on the baking sheet, lift out the liner and weights. Transfer the pan to a wire rack and let the shell come to room temperature.

Reduce the oven temperature to 300°F. Place the tomato purée, goat cheese, eggs, kosher salt, and Tabasco in a blender and blend until frothy.

Place the cooled tart shell in its pan on a rimmed baking sheet. Pour in about half the tomato filling; pour the rest into a small pitcher. Move the tart to the oven, then fill nearly to the top with the filling from the pitcher. Be careful not to overflow, or the tart could be hard to remove; you may not use all the filling.

Bake until just set, about 45 minutes; rotate the pan halfway through. The tart is done when a knife inserted in the center comes out clean. Set on a wire rack to cool somewhat.

Once cool enough to handle, remove the ring and set the tart on a serving plate. Cut tomatoes in halves or quarters; leave very small varieties whole. Garnish around the edges with the tomatoes and whole basil leaves. Sprinkle with sea salt.

Slice and serve with extra-virgin olive oil and balsamic vinegar, if you wish, for drizzling.

NOTE

You can certainly use canned purée—but I wouldn't complain if you made your own. It's easy, too. Peel and seed very good tomatoes, then whirl away in a blender with just enough water to get them moving. The purée may need a touch of vinegar and a pinch of sugar, depending on your tomatoes.

Artichoke Clafouti

The 1970s was when my food awareness began to develop. My mother was a fantastic cook. She probably acquired most of her skills during this same period, and I'd bet that Julia Child and the whole Mastering the Art of French Cooking *craze were her primary sources of inspiration. While other kids were scarfing down Tuna Twist, Mug-O-Lunch, and Shake-A-Pudd'n, my mom was serving us Bouillabaisse, Duck à l'Orange, and Mousse de Foies de Volaille. She even taught my little brother and me how to make perfect little crêpes so that she could have 2 or 3 pans going at once for her famous dinner parties. This artichoke clafouti recipe comes from that time in my life. It's my mother's recipe, essentially a crustless quiche—which feels intensely modern to me.*

MAKES 6 SIDE DISH OR 4 LIGHT MAIN COURSE SERVINGS

½ cup plus 1 tablespoon olive oil, divided

¼ cup freshly squeezed lemon juice

2 teaspoons grated lemon zest

2 cloves garlic, minced

1 tablespoon plus 1 teaspoon minced fresh thyme leaves

1 bay leaf

Kosher salt and freshly cracked pepper

1 (14-ounce) can quartered artichoke hearts, drained

1 small red bell pepper, cut into ⅛-inch dice (about 1 cup)

1 small yellow bell pepper, cut into ⅛-inch dice (about 1 cup)

1 small zucchini, cut into ⅛-inch dice (about 1 cup)

4 green onions (white, light green, and some dark green parts), thinly sliced

2 anchovies fillets, minced (optional)

1 teaspoon unsalted butter, at room temperature

2 tablespoons dried Italian-style breadcrumbs

4 large eggs

⅔ cup half and half

½ cup all-purpose flour

½ cup grated Parmesan cheese

Place an oven rack in the center position. Preheat the oven to 375°F.

In a shallow baking dish, stir together ½ cup olive oil, lemon juice, lemon zest, garlic, 1 tablespoon thyme, bay leaf, and a big pinch each of salt and pepper. Add the artichokes, stirring to coat with the oil mixture. Roast until the artichokes are browned in spots and very tender when pierced with a knife, about 25 minutes. Remove from oven and let cool. Lower the oven temperature to 300°F.

Remove the bay leaf and drain the cooled artichokes. Set aside.

Heat the remaining 1 tablespoon olive oil in a large skillet over medium-high heat. Add the red and yellow bell pepper, zucchini, green onions, remaining 1 teaspoon thyme, and a pinch each of salt and pepper. Cook, stirring occasionally, until the vegetables are softened and beginning to color, about 8 minutes. Turn off the heat and stir in the roasted artichokes and minced anchovies, if using; set aside to cool. (The dish may be made up to 2 days ahead to this point and refrigerated, covered.)

Butter the bottom and sides of a shallow 1½-quart glass or ceramic baking dish or 9-inch pie pan. Dust with the breadcrumbs, shaking out the excess. Set on a rimmed baking sheet and spoon in the cooled vegetables, spreading evenly.

Break the eggs into a medium bowl and whisk in the half and half, flour, and a pinch each of salt and pepper. Whisk vigorously until tiny bubbles are suspended in the mixture; stir in the Parmesan. Pour over the vegetables. Carefully move the baking sheet to the oven. Bake until the filling is just set and a knife inserted in the center comes out clean, about 45 minutes. Serve warm or at room temperature.

> **NOTE**
>
> Choose canned or frozen artichokes, not the marinated jarred variety. You can also use fresh baby artichokes, trimmed and pared down, with the thistles removed. In that case, increase the roasting time by about 15 minutes.

Broccolini Tart with Cherry Tomatoes, Feta, and Fried Garlic

Is broccolini related to rapini? Or is it just baby broccoli? Actually, it's neither. It's an ingenious cross between standard broccoli and Chinese broccoli. Its presence on the plate and even the name are reminiscent of the Italian staple rapini (broccoli rabe), without that annoying bitter edge most kids and even some adults won't go near. It's a rather new invention—if food can be an invention. Broccolini is, in fact, a trademarked brand name—if vegetables can have brand names.

MAKES 6 SERVINGS

Basic Pie Pastry (page 16)*

1 teaspoon coarsely cracked black pepper, plus more as needed

½ cup olive oil

3 cloves garlic, thinly sliced

1 pound broccolini, ends trimmed

Flour for rolling

¼ cup finely grated Parmesan cheese

18 small cherry or grape tomatoes (about ⅓ pound)

3 ounces crumbled feta

¼ teaspoon red pepper flakes

Kosher salt

1 large egg yolk lightly beaten with 1 teaspoon water, for egg wash

* Other choices: Cream Cheese Crust (page 17), Extra-Rich Short Pastry (page 19), and Gluten-Free Pie Pastry (page 20).

Prepare the pastry recipe, adding 1 teaspoon cracked black pepper with the flour. Shape the dough into 2 discs ¾ inch thick—one about 7 inches in diameter, the other about 3 inches in diameter. Wrap in plastic and refrigerate at least 1 hour (or up to 2 days), or freeze for up to 1 month.

In a small saucepan over medium heat, heat the olive oil. Add 1 garlic slice to the hot oil, it should bubble; if so, add the remaining garlic. Cook, swirling the pan often, until the garlic just begins to color on the edges, about 1 minute more. Don't let it get too brown—it will continue to cook in the hot oil. Set aside.

Bring a large pot of salted water to a boil. Add the broccolini and blanch about 2 minutes. Using tongs, transfer while still bright green to a paper towel–lined plate. Pat dry with more paper towels.

On a lightly floured surface, use a lightly floured rolling pin to shape the larger dough disc into about a 12 x 15-inch rectangle, a generous ⅛ inch thick. Carefully fold in half crosswise, slide onto the rolling pin, and transfer to a parchment-lined baking sheet. Unfold and center the dough. If it tears, gently repair it with scraps.

Sprinkle with Parmesan and arrange the broccolini evenly on the dough in an attractive, casual manner, leaving a 2-inch border all around. Nestle the tomatoes into the broccolini here and there. Top with feta and red pepper and drizzle with 2 tablespoons of the infused oil from the fried garlic. Season lightly with a pinch each of salt and pepper. Fold the dough border casually over the filling without stretching it. Let it drape and fall where it will; it won't cover all the filling.

Brush the exposed dough with egg wash. Refrigerate until chilled, about 20 minutes. Meanwhile, place an oven rack in the center position and preheat the oven to 400°F.

Bake the chilled tart until the crust is golden, the tomatoes begin to pucker, and the feta starts to color, about 30 minutes. Serve warm or at room temperature, topped with fried garlic slices and a drizzle of garlic-infused oil.

Lattice-Topped Mushroom Pie

It may seem redundant to roast the mushrooms before you bake them for nearly an hour inside this pie. You might even be worried that I'm instructing you to overcook these beauties. But the truth is, roasting intensifies their deep, earthy nature. It also lets them weep out their moisture, making them meatier and denser. Don't worry that they'll be too dry—the roasted mushrooms in this pie are swimming in a creamy, cheesy sauce that's flavorful enough to save almost any cooking disaster. So roast away.

MAKES 6 TO 8 SERVINGS

Basic Pie Pastry (page 16)*

3 pounds assorted mushrooms (such as cremini, shitake, and chanterelle), cut into bite-size pieces

½ cup olive oil

1 teaspoon kosher salt, plus more as needed

¼ teaspoon freshly cracked black pepper, plus more as needed

3 tablespoons unsalted butter

3 tablespoons all-purpose flour, plus more for rolling

1¼ cups whole milk, divided

4 ounces Taleggio cheese, grated

4 ounces fontina cheese, grated

2 tablespoons minced fresh thyme leaves

4 ounces low-moisture mozzarella cheese, cut into ½-inch dice

1 large egg yolk lightly beaten with 1 teaspoon water, for egg wash

* Other choices: Cream Cheese Crust (page 17), Extra-Rich Short Pastry (page 19), and Gluten-Free Pie Pastry (page 20).

Prepare the pastry and shape it into 2 discs ¾ inch thick—one about 6 inches in diameter, the other about 4 inches in diameter. Wrap in plastic and refrigerate at least 1 hour (or up to 2 days), or freeze for up to 1 month.

Place an oven rack in the center position. Preheat the oven to 400°F. In a large bowl, toss the mushrooms with the olive oil, 1 teaspoon salt, and ¼ teaspoon pepper. Spread on a rimmed, parchment-lined baking sheet in as close to a single layer as possible; use a second sheet if necessary. Roast until slightly browned, about 18 to 20 minutes. Let cool completely.

In a medium saucepan, melt the butter over medium heat. Whisk in flour until a paste forms. Gradually pour in ¼ cup milk, whisking until a paste begins to be released from the bottom. Reduce the heat and add the remaining 1 cup milk and any accumulated mushroom juices. Cook until thickened, whisking often, about 5 minutes. Remove from the heat and stir in the Taleggio and fontina until melted, followed by the thyme. Season with a pinch each of salt and pepper. Stir in the mushrooms. Set aside to cool.

On a lightly floured surface, use a lightly floured rolling pin to roll the larger dough disc to about a 13-inch round, a generous ⅛ inch thick. Carefully fold in half, slide onto the rolling pin, and transfer to a 9-inch deep-dish or 10-inch standard pie pan. Unfold, easing the dough gently into the pan without stretching it. Let the excess drape over the sides.

Spread the cooled mushroom mixture in the pie shell. Sprinkle mozzarella evenly on top. Brush the rim with egg wash.

On a freshly floured surface, use a freshly floured rolling pin to roll the second dough disc to a square about 10 x 10 inches and a generous ⅛ inch thick. Using a pizza wheel or paring knife, cut into 10 or 11 strips about ¾ inch wide.

Starting 1 inch from the edge of the pan, lay 5 strips vertically across the filling at about 1-inch intervals. Fold the second and fourth strips back a bit more than halfway over themselves. Place a sixth strip horizontally across the 3 strips at the center of the pie, then unfold the other strips. Next fold back the first, third, and fifth vertical strips and place a seventh strip about 1 inch above the horizontal center strip; unfold the folded strips. Fold back the second and fourth strips. Lay an eighth strip horizontally about 1 inch above the previous one; unfold the folded strips. Repeat below the center horizontal strip to complete the lattice.

Trim, leaving a ½-inch overhang, then turn under and press the edges together; flute or crimp decoratively. Refrigerate until chilled, about 20 minutes. Meanwhile, place an oven rack in the center position and preheat the oven to 400°F.

Brush the remaining egg wash over the exposed dough. Bake until the pastry is crisp and golden, about 50 minutes. Let cool on a rack at least 15 minutes before slicing. Serve warm or at room temperature.

❧ WINE PAIRING

Buttery Chardonnay from California, preferably the Napa or Sonoma region.

With rich flavors of ripe pear and subtle vanilla, Chardonnay has a velvety texture that's a great match for the creamy, cheesy Mornay sauce in this pie. A touch of oakiness pairs well with the earthy mushroom flavors, and the wine's buttery component is nice with the flaky and abundant crust. Recommended producers: Hansel, Domaine Georg Rafael, Acacia.

Flamiche

Flamiche is the Flemish word for cake. So how did it find its way into a pie book? Once upon a time, flamiche was typically seen wrapped in a yeast-based dough—making it a bit more cake-like, I suppose. But it's a pie in my mind, because today it's most often baked inside a pastry crust. I've seen it served in an open tart shell or with a double crust, as in this recipe. In either case, it's a specialty of the Picardy region in northern France.

MAKES 6 TO 8 SERVINGS

Basic Pie Pastry (page 16)*

1 teaspoon white vinegar

Flour for rolling

2 tablespoons unsalted butter

4 leeks (white and light green parts), thinly sliced (about 1 pound after slicing)

Kosher salt and white pepper

8 ounces semisoft cow's-milk cheese (such as Port Salut, Morbier, or even fontina), grated

1 egg, lightly beaten

1 egg yolk

¼ cup half and half, plus more for brushing

* Other choices: Cream Cheese Crust (page 17), Extra-Rich Short Pastry (page 19), and Gluten-Free Pie Pastry (page 20).

Prepare the pastry recipe, replacing some of the water with 1 teaspoon white vinegar. Shape the dough into 2 discs about 5 inches in diameter and ¾ inch thick. Wrap in plastic and refrigerate at least 1 hour (or up to 2 days), or freeze for up to 1 month.

On a lightly floured surface, use a lightly floured rolling pin to roll 1 dough disc to an 11 or 12-inch round, a generous ⅛ inch thick. Carefully fold in half, slide onto the rolling pin, and transfer to a 9-inch fluted tart pan with removable bottom. Gently press to line the pan without stretching or tearing. Use light pressure to push the dough into the sides, letting the excess drape over. Repair any holes with a bit of extra dough. Chill the dough-lined pan while you make the filling.

Place an oven rack in the center position. Preheat the oven to 375°F.

Melt the butter in a large saucepan over medium heat. Add the sliced leeks and a generous pinch of salt. Cook, stirring often, until the leeks are quite softened but aren't yet coloring, about 10 minutes. Stir in the cheese and a pinch of white pepper. When the cheese is melted, set it aside to cool completely.

In a large bowl, whisk together the egg, egg yolk, and ¼ cup half and half. Stir in the cooled leek mixture and a bit more salt and white pepper. Pour into the lined tart pan and spread evenly.

On a freshly floured surface, use a freshly floured rolling pin to roll the remaining chilled dough disc to a large round, a generous ⅛ inch thick. Cut a ½-inch hole in the center. Carefully fold in half, slide onto the rolling pin, and transfer to cover the tart. Press to seal the crust at the edge of the pan; run a rolling pin over the top to neatly trim. Brush the exposed dough with more half and half. Set on a rimmed baking sheet and bake until lightly golden, about 45 minutes. Let rest on a rack at least 10 minutes before removing the tart ring. Slice and serve warm or at room temperature.

Arugula, Black Olive, and Sun-Dried Tomato Calzone

Calzones offer all the perks of pizza, but they hold way more stuff. Cheese, especially. You can pack more cheese into a single calzone than you can pile on top of the most colossal pizza imaginable. Yes, that's hyperbole—but just like pizza, calzones are the perfect vehicle for just about any ingredient you crave. I chose a combination of arugula and black olives, then added some chewy, oil-packed sun-dried tomatoes as a sweetly surprising contrast to all that cheese.

MAKES 2 LARGE CALZONES, 2 TO 4 SERVINGS

1½ pounds Easy Flatbread Dough (page 18) or purchased pizza dough cornmeal for pizza stone

Flour for rolling

1 cup well-drained fresh ricotta, divided

Kosher salt and freshly cracked black pepper

2 cups lightly packed arugula leaves, divided

½ cup pitted and halved jarred kalamata or black olives, divided

½ cup oil-packed sun-dried tomatoes, drained and coarsely chopped, divided

6 ounces sliced low-moisture mozzarella cheese, divided

2 tablespoons finely grated Parmesan cheese, divided, plus more for topping

Red pepper flakes, as needed (optional)

Olive oil, as needed

Dried oregano, to taste

Marinara sauce, to serve

Prepare the dough recipe; I prefer water to milk for this recipe, but either is fine. Lay the dough on a lightly floured surface and knead gently 3 or 4 times. Divide in half and flatten into 2 discs with the palm of your hand. Sprinkle lightly with flour, cover, and let rest at least 15 minutes. This will relax the dough, making it easier to roll or stretch.

Sprinkle a little cornmeal onto a pizza stone. Place on the lowest rack of a cold oven. Turn the oven to its highest temperature, about 500°F. You want the stone very hot, so leave ample time for it to heat through. (I like the pizza stone from King Arthur Flour, measuring ½ x 14½ x 16½ inches.)

On a lightly floured surface, roll or stretch the rested dough into two 10 or 11-inch rounds about ⅓ inch thick. Cover and let rest at least 15 minutes. If the dough rounds have retracted after resting, use your fingertips to return them to about 10 inches in diameter.

Spread half the ricotta onto 1 side of each dough round, leaving a ¾-inch border. Sprinkle with a pinch each of salt and pepper. Heap half the arugula, black olives, and sun-dried tomatoes on top, followed by half the mozzarella. Sprinkle with 1 tablespoon Parmesan and a pinch of red pepper, if using. Brush the outer edge with water and fold the dough over to enclose the filling, forming a half-moon. Roll the edges in slightly with your fingers, then crimp to seal. Use your fingers or fork tines to create a decorative edge, if you like. Trim and discard the excess dough creating a neat ⅓-inch rim. Leave as a half-moon or pull the 2 ends together, pinching them where they meet, to a form a circle. (I like the folds and undulations this forms, making for an interestingly textured crust.) Transfer to an oiled, rimless, or upside-down baking sheet, reshaping the calzones if needed. Brush with olive oil.

❧ WINE PAIRING

Dry rosé, preferably from southern France.

With bright red flavors of strawberry, racy acidity, and an almost imperceptible sweetness, rosés exhibit both red wine and white wine characteristics. I love rosé with sun-dried tomatoes, olives, and almost every other food from the Mediterranean palette. Rosés are best when made from 100% red wine grapes. Recommended producers: Trinquevedel, Domaine de la Mordorée, E. Guigal.

Quickly and carefully slide the calzones onto the hot pizza stone in oven. Don't crowd them; if necessary, bake them separately. Bake until deeply golden, 12 to 15 minutes depending on your oven's temperature. Leave the hot stone in the oven and use tongs to carefully slide each calzone onto a plate or cutting board. Let rest about 10 minutes, then top as you like with Parmesan, red pepper, and dried oregano. Serve hot with marinara on the side.

NOTE

If you have a pizza peel, feel free to use that instead of a greased upside-down baking sheet. Then again, if you have a pizza peel you probably don't need my advice, anyway.

Fresh Tomato Pie with Corn Cracker Crust

Every cook in the South has some version of this recipe, so it's hard to say exactly what's correct. Mine is inspired by memories of sitting in the blazing hot shade on a porch in Georgia. I gave my pie a cornmeal crust, because cornbread and Georgia go together like tomatoes and summer.

MAKES 6 TO 8 SERVINGS

Corn Cracker Crust

1½ cups (187 grams) all-purpose flour, plus more for rolling

½ cup (80 grams) yellow cornmeal

1 tablespoon granulated sugar

½ teaspoon baking powder

½ teaspoon baking soda

½ teaspoon kosher salt, divided, plus more as needed

Pinch of cayenne pepper (optional)

½ cup (1 stick) chilled unsalted butter, cut into ½-inch cubes

1 large egg, lightly beaten

1 large egg yolk, lightly beaten

¼ cup heavy cream

Note: Other crust choices for this pie include Basic Pie Pastry (page 16), Cream Cheese Crust (page 17), Extra-Rich Short Pastry (page 19), and Gluten-Free Pie Pastry (page 20).

Tomato Filling

5 large, ripe tomatoes (about 2 pounds), ends removed, cut crosswise into 4 slices each

½ teaspoon kosher salt, plus more for tomatoes

1 tablespoon grated Parmesan cheese

½ cup mayonnaise

2 green onions (white, light green, and some dark green parts), thinly sliced

2 tablespoons chopped fresh dill

1 tablespoon apple cider vinegar

2 teaspoons brown sugar

1 teaspoon mustard seeds

1 teaspoon celery seeds

½ teaspoon freshly ground black pepper, plus more as needed

2½ cups coarsely grated extra-sharp Cheddar cheese, divided

To make the crust, in the bowl of a food processor pulse the 1½ cups flour, cornmeal, sugar, baking powder, baking soda, 1 teaspoon salt, and cayenne (if using) 5 or 6 times until well combined. Add the butter and process about 6 to 8 seconds, until the mixture is crumbly and coarse, with small chunks of butter visible throughout. Add the egg, egg yolk, and cream. Process until the dough just comes together and begins to pull away from the sides, about 15 seconds.

On a lightly floured work surface, gently knead the dough 2 or 3 times. If it seems quite sticky, sprinkle in another teaspoon or so of flour and give a couple more quick, gentle kneads. Shape into a disc about 8 inches across and ¾ inch thick. Wrap in plastic and refrigerate at least 1 hour (or up to 2 days), or freeze for up to 1 month.

To fill the pie, while the dough chills remove as many seeds from the tomato slices as possible. Line 2 large baking sheets with a double layer of paper towels. Spread the tomatoes on top in a single layer and sprinkle lightly with salt. Place another double layer of paper towels over the tomatoes and set another baking sheet on top as a weight; let stand for 15 minutes. Replace the wet paper towels with dry layers and repeat the process for 15 or 20 more minutes—too much juice can ruin this pie.

Butter the bottom and sides of a standard 10-inch pie pan (1½ to 2 quarts); sprinkle with Parmesan, letting it adhere to the bottom and sides. Set aside.

On a lightly floured surface, use a lightly floured rolling pin to roll the chilled dough to a 12 or 13-inch round, about ¼ inch thick. (It can be helpful to roll this dough between sheets of parchment or waxed paper.) Carefully fold in half, slide onto the rolling pin, and transfer to the pie pan. If the dough breaks (and it probably will, because it can be quite crumbly), push it back together with your fingers; trim the edge neatly or rustically, as you see fit. Cover and refrigerate until chilled, about 20 minutes.

Place an oven rack in the center position. Preheat the oven to 375°F.

In a small bowl, mix together the mayonnaise, green onions, dill, vinegar, brown sugar, mustard seeds, celery seeds, ½ teaspoon salt, and ½ teaspoon black pepper.

Spread 1 cup of the grated Cheddar in the dough-lined pan. Cover the bottom with 9 tomato slices, overlapping slightly if necessary. Use a rubber spatula to spread about half the mayonnaise mixture on top. Repeat, layering another 1 cup Cheddar, 11 tomato slices, and the remaining mayonnaise mixture. Sprinkle the remaining ½ cup Cheddar on top. Season with salt and pepper.

Bake until the crust and cheese are golden brown, about 25 minutes. You may need to cover the crust edges with strips of foil during the last 10 minutes to keep them from getting too brown. This is a picnic pie, so let it come to room temperature before slicing it. It should not be served less than 2 or 3 hours after baking. But may be served up to 24 hours after baking. Refrigerate and return to room temperature if serving time is more than 3 hours after baking.

Apple Endive Tart with Candied Pecans

I hope you love endive as much as I do. I was first introduced to in the 1970s and early '80s. It seemed rather exotic and expensive to me then. The heads came from the store preciously packed between blue sheets of paper—creamy white, pointy-looking things. What were they, I wondered, some sort of flower bud? To this grade school geek, they seemed like something from another planet. I've long since seen the light. Endive has a natural bitterness that's quite complex. It's a terrific complement to bold and/or creamy flavors, and this tart is loaded with both.

MAKES 12 SLICES

¼ cup sugar

¼ teaspoon freshly cracked black pepper, plus more as needed

1 teaspoon water

¾ cup pecan halves, lightly toasted

¼ teaspoon kosher salt

Flour for rolling

1 (14-ounce) package frozen all-butter puff pastry, thawed in the refrigerator*

2 tablespoons unsalted butter

4 heads Belgian endive, cored and roughly chopped

½ cup coarsely chopped shallots

3 tart apples (such as Granny Smith), peeled, cored, and coarsely chopped

2 tablespoons apple cider vinegar

4 ounces crumbled blue cheese

2 tablespoons coarsely chopped fresh chives

1 egg yolk lightly beaten with 1 teaspoon water, for egg wash

* Two sheets from a 17.3-ounce package of puff pastry can be stacked, folded, and rolled together as a substitute for the 14-ounce package listed above; you'll have pastry left over.

Line a rimmed baking sheet with parchment paper. Set aside.

In a medium heavy-bottomed saucepan over medium heat, cook the sugar, pepper, and water, stirring constantly with a wooden spoon. Once the sugar melts and begins to turn amber, add the pecans. Work quickly, stirring to coat each piece with the melted sugar mixture. Quickly spread the nuts on the prepared baking sheet, using a fork to separate them. Be careful—the melted sugar will be very hot. Sprinkle with the salt while still warm. Let cool completely. (The nuts can be made up to 2 days ahead and stored, covered, at room temperature.)

Line another baking sheet with parchment. On a lightly floured surface, use a lightly floured rolling pin to roll the puff pastry to about a 10 x 15-inch rectangle, a scant ¼ inch thick. Cut in half lengthwise, giving you two 15 x 5-inch rectangles. Carefully transfer them side by side to the prepared baking sheet. (You can also bake them on separate sheets, or even at different times.)

Use a ruler and a sharp knife to trim the edges of 1 rectangle and lightly score the pastry ½ inch in from the edges to mark a border; don't cut all the way through. Use a fork to prick the pastry at half-inch intervals inside the border. Repeat with the second rectangle. Refrigerate until chilled, about 20 minutes. Meanwhile, place an oven rack in the center position and preheat the oven to 400°F.

Bake the pastry until barely golden, 8 to 10 minutes. Pop any large air bubbles and use a small, flat spatula to flatten the bottom, but not the rim. You may need to run a knife along the score line to assist in the flattening process.

Melt the butter in a large cast-iron or other heavy-bottomed skillet over medium-high heat. Add the chopped endive and shallots and sauté until softened and just beginning to color, about 8 minutes. Add the apples and vinegar; cook until tender, about 4 minutes. Remove from the heat and stir in the blue cheese and chives. Scoop half of the mixture onto each tart shell, spreading it evenly and keeping it inside the rim. Brush the rims with egg wash.

Bake until the crust is nicely browned and the filling is bubbling, about 15 minutes. Begin checking at about 12 minutes to make sure the crust doesn't get too brown. Set on a rack to cool for at least 10 minutes. Transfer to serving plate(s) and sprinkle with the candied pecans. Slice and serve warm or at room temperature with a generous grinding of coarsely ground black pepper.

Penang Vegetable Curry Pot Pie

There are so many curries from so many different cultures, I felt the need to qualify this one with the name Penang. Sometimes spelled "Phanaeng," this style is generally milder than other Thai curries. Not that I let that stop me from slipping in a couple teaspoons of Sriracha.

MAKES 6

2 tablespoons vegetable oil

2 medium shallots, minced (about ½ cup)

2 cloves garlic, minced

4 tablespoons red curry paste, or more to taste

2 teaspoons Sriracha hot sauce (optional)

1 (3-inch) piece fresh ginger peeled and grated (about 2 tablespoons)

1 (3-inch) piece fresh lemongrass, outer layers removed, minced (about 1 tablespoon)

1 (14-ounce) can unsweetened coconut milk

1½ cups vegetable broth

1 tablespoon sugar

2 tablespoons fish sauce, or more to taste (optional)

6 Kaffir lime leaves, crinkled to release the oils, often available in Asian markets (or the finely grated zest of 1 lime)

2 tablespoons cornstarch

¼ cup water

2 carrots, peeled and cut into ½-inch dice (about 1 cup)

1 bell pepper, cut into ½-inch dice (about 2 cups)

8 ounces extra-firm tofu, cut into ½-inch dice

1 cup loosely packed basil leaves

Juice of 1 lime

1 cup frozen peas

1 (7.4-ounce) can straw mushrooms, drained

Kosher salt and freshly cracked black pepper

Flour for rolling

1 (14-ounce) package frozen all-butter puff pastry, thawed in the refrigerator*

1 large egg yolk lightly beaten with 1 teaspoon water, for egg wash

* Two sheets from a 17.3-ounce package of puff pastry can be stacked, folded, and rolled together as a substitute for the 14-ounce package listed above; you'll have pastry left over.

Heat the vegetable oil in a large sauté pan over medium-high heat. Stir in the shallots and garlic. Cook, stirring often, until the shallots are tender, about 2 minutes. Add the curry paste and Sriracha, if using; cook for a minute more. Stir in the ginger and lemongrass; cook for another minute. Add the coconut milk, vegetable broth, sugar, fish sauce, if using, and lime leaves or zest. Bring to a boil, then reduce to a gentle simmer.

Meanwhile, in a small cup stir the cornstarch into the water to create a slurry. Add to the simmering curry along with the carrots and bell pepper. Continue to simmer until the liquid thickens, stirring occasionally, about 10 minutes. Remove and gently stir in the tofu, basil leaves, lime juice, peas, and straw mushrooms. Season with salt and pepper as needed. Allow to come to room temperature. (The filling may be made up to 2 days ahead and refrigerated, covered. Let return to room temperature before continuing.)

Divide the cooled curry mixture evenly among six 1-cup ramekins. It should come almost to the brim.

On a lightly floured work surface, use a lightly floured rolling pin to roll the puff pastry to a 10 x 15-inch rectangle, a scant ¼ inch thick. Use a cutter or template 1 inch larger all around than your ramekins to make 6 dough rounds, folding and re-rolling scraps if necessary. Place on a parchment-lined baking sheet and refrigerate until chilled, about 20 minutes.

Meanwhile, place an oven rack in the center position. Preheat the oven to 425°F.

Brush the outside rim of each filled ramekin with egg wash. Place a chilled pastry round on top of each, allowing the excess to drape over evenly. Brush the tops with more egg wash. Transfer to a rimmed baking sheet and bake until the pastry is puffed and golden brown, 20 to 25 minutes. Serve hot.

❧ WINE PAIRING

German Riesling, preferably Spätlese, from the Mosel region.

Subtly flavored with nectarine, apricot, and green apple, underscored by slatey earth notes, Riesling is arguably the most versatile white wine. With delicate flavors and light body, it doesn't overpower the vegetables in this pie, and its slight sweetness and balanced acidity complement the exotic curry and coconut flavors. Recommended producers: J.J. Prüm, Dr. H. Thanisch, Dr. Loosen.

HAND PIES

Crawfish and Corn Turnovers

When people begin making an association between a place and a meal, or a restaurant and a certain dish, magic happens. Icons are created. Often these connections involve the simplest foods, local dishes served for generations. To me, crawfish is one of those foods. It belongs so completely to New Orleans that I rarely even consider it in my day-to-day life. So I asked my friend Gisele Perez—NOLA expat, fellow blogger (www.painperdublog.com), and professional chef—how she'd serve crawfish baked in a pie. She came up with these turnovers. Pure NOLA with a touch of Creole sophistication. You'll have leftover filling, and that's by design, as it freezes well.

MAKES 36

Cream Cheese Crust (page 17)*

5 tablespoons unsalted butter, divided

2 tablespoons finely diced celery

½ cup finely diced onion

2 tablespoons finely diced red bell pepper

¾ teaspoon dried thyme

1 clove garlic, minced

½ teaspoon freshly cracked black pepper

¼ teaspoon cayenne pepper, or to taste

½ teaspoon kosher salt

1 cup sautéed fresh corn kernels, from 1 large ear

3 tablespoons minced green onions (white and light green parts only)

3 tablespoons minced fresh flat-leaf parsley

1 pound crawfish tails, washed, drained, and dried with a paper towel

1 tablespoon brandy

1½ teaspoons tomato paste

2 ounces cream cheese

Flour for rolling

2 egg yolks mixed with 2 teaspoons water, for egg wash

* Other choices: Basic Pie Pastry (page 16), Extra-Rich Short Pastry (page 19), and Gluten-Free Pie Pastry (page 20).

Prepare the dough for the crust and shape it into 2 discs about 5 inches in diameter and ¾ inch thick. Wrap in plastic and refrigerate at least 1 hour (or up to 2 days), or freeze for up to 1 month.

Melt 3 tablespoons butter in a large sauté pan over medium heat. When the foam subsides, add the celery, onions, bell pepper, and thyme. Cook, stirring occasionally, until softened, about 4 minutes. Stir in the garlic, black pepper, cayenne, and salt and cook a minute or so more. Stir in the corn kernels, green onions, and parsley. Remove from the heat.

Melt the remaining 2 tablespoons butter in another large sauté pan over high heat. When it begins to bubble, add the crawfish tails and sauté them quickly, about 1 minute.

Remove from the burner and add the brandy. Ignite, let the flames die, and return to the heat. Cook, stirring often, until the liquid has evaporated. Add the tomato paste and cream cheese, stirring until the cream cheese is melted. Adjust the seasoning with a pinch each of salt and pepper, if needed. Remove from the heat and let cool. Cover and refrigerate until chilled, at least 1 hour or as long as overnight. (You can also freeze the cooled filling, covered, for up to 1 month.)

On a lightly floured surface, use a lightly floured rolling pin to roll 1 chilled dough disc into a large round a scant ⅛ inch thick. Use a 3½-inch cutter to cut about 18 circles of dough, re-rolling the scraps if necessary. Transfer to a parchment-lined baking sheet. Repeat with the second dough disc and a second parchment-lined baking sheet. Cover with plastic wrap and chill on the baking sheets for about 20 minutes.

Place 2 teaspoons filling in the center of each dough round. Don't overfill, or they'll be difficult to seal. Moisten the edges with a little egg wash, using your finger. Fold into a half-moon; press the edges together and crimp or roll decoratively. Cover and refrigerate until chilled, at least 20 minutes but no more than 1 hour before baking. (These can also be frozen for up to a month, tightly covered in a single layer, and then baked while still frozen.)

Meanwhile, place oven racks in upper and center positions and preheat the oven to 400°F.

Brush egg wash on the tops of the chilled turnovers. Bake until golden brown, 25 to 30 minutes; switch the sheets halfway through. Remove from the baking sheets to cool on racks for 10 minutes. Serve warm.

❧ WINE PAIRING

Chardonnay from Burgundy, preferably with little to no oak.

Typically medium-bodied with bright apple, pear, and citrus flavors and a stony minerality, this is not your big, buttery Chardonnay. The firm acidity in the wine heightens the sweetness of the crawfish, corn, and tomato paste and highlights the earthiness in the peppers, onions, and garlic. I find Old World Chardonnay to be extremely food-friendly. Recommended producers: Jean-Marc Brocard, Château de Fuissé, Domaine Oliver Leflaive.

Leftover Pot Roast Hand Pies with Cheddar

There's always leftover pot roast. Always. There's always leftover turkey, too, and this recipe could just as easily be made with that—in which case I'd change the cheese to Jarlsberg. But I had leftover pot roast, so pot roast it is. That's how leftovers are. They refuse to be ignored.

MAKES 8

Basic Pie Pastry (page 16)*

8 ounces leftover cooked pot roast

1 cup vegetable broth

2 teaspoons minced fresh thyme leaves, divided

1 bay leaf

1 teaspoon sherry vinegar

Flour for rolling

Kosher salt and freshly cracked black pepper

2 ounces Cheddar cheese (as sharp as you like), cut into ¼-inch dice

1 egg yolk lightly beaten with 1 teaspoon water, for egg wash

* Other choices: Cream Cheese Crust (page 17), Extra-Rich Short Pastry (page 19), and Gluten-Free Pie Pastry (page 20).

Prepare the pastry dough and shape it into 2 discs about 5 inches in diameter and ¾ inch thick. Wrap in plastic and refrigerate at least 1 hour (or up to 2 days), or freeze for up to 1 month.

Use 2 forks to shred the meat. Place the meat, vegetable broth, 1 teaspoon thyme, and bay leaf in a medium saucepan over medium-high heat. Bring to a boil, then reduce the heat, cover, and simmer about 20 minutes, stirring several times with a wooden spoon to break up the meat. Uncover the pan, remove the bay leaf, and add the vinegar. Increase to medium heat and cook, stirring often, until the liquid is nearly evaporated and the

🌿 WINE PAIRING

Merlot and Merlot blends from Washington.

Bursting with blackberry, blueberry, and dark plum flavors, Merlot is similar to but often softer than Cabernet Sauvignon. This is still a full-bodied wine, however, and holds its own next to braised beef. I think Merlot is ideal with medium-flavored cheeses such as Cheddar, and the pie's thyme links up with the wine's herbal notes. Recommended producers: Andrew Will, Canoe Ridge, Columbia Crest.

meat is well stewed, about 20 minutes. Drain in a colander set in the sink. Allow the meat to come to room temperature.

On a lightly floured surface, use a lightly floured rolling pin to roll 1 chilled dough disc to a generous ⅛-inch thickness. Using a round cutter or a plate as a template, cut into four 5-inch rounds. Transfer to a parchment-lined baking sheet, evenly spaced and not touching. Repeat with the remaining dough, giving you 8 rounds on 2 sheets. Refrigerate until chilled, about 20 minutes.

Place oven racks in the center and upper positions. Preheat the oven to 425°F.

Divide the meat evenly among the chilled rounds, leaving about a ¾-inch border. Season lightly with salt and pepper and top with Cheddar cubes. Fold the edges inward to create a triangular shape—a bit like George Washington's hat. The edges shouldn't meet in the middle but should be sealed shut at the 3 points where they form corners. Brush the dough with egg wash and sprinkle with the remaining 1 teaspoon thyme.

Bake until the pies are golden brown, about 30 minutes; switch sheets halfway through. Cool slightly on a wire rack and serve warm.

Jerk-Spiced Meat Patties with Mango Habanero Hot Sauce

There's a lot of flavor packed into these little pies. You can make them as spicy as you like by using as much of the minced habanero as you dare. Sure, habaneros are hot. But they're more nuanced than a lot of chiles, with complex floral notes that partner perfectly with sweet mangoes. So be brave. I like this fairly spicy, so I add a whole habanero to both the hot sauce and the filling.

If you prefer to leave out the rum, you can substitute ½ cup water mixed with about 1 tablespoon dark brown sugar for that all-important sweet element.

MAKES 8

Basic Pie Pastry (page 16)*

2 teaspoons West Indian or Madras-style hot curry powder, divided

2 medium onions (about 1 pound)

1 medium carrot (about ¼ pound)

2 tablespoons vegetable oil, divided

6 cloves garlic, minced, divided

2 or 3 small, very ripe mangoes (such as Ataulfo), peeled and coarsely chopped

1 or 2 habanero chiles, seeded and minced, divided

1 cup apple cider vinegar

1¼ cups mango or orange juice, or as needed

Kosher salt

1-inch piece of fresh ginger, peeled and grated

8 ounces ground pork

8 ounces ground beef

1 teaspoon ground coriander

½ teaspoon ground cumin

½ teaspoon ground allspice

⅛ teaspoon ground cloves

1 tablespoon minced fresh thyme leaves

½ cup dark rum

Flour for rolling

1 egg lightly beaten with 1 teaspoon water, for egg wash

* Other choices: Cream Cheese Crust (page 17), Extra-Rich Short Pastry (page 19), and Gluten-Free Pie Pastry (page 20).

Prepare the pastry recipe, adding 1 teaspoon curry powder to the flour mixture. Shape the dough into two 5-inch squares about ¾ inch thick. Wrap in plastic and refrigerate at least 1 hour (or up to 2 days), or freeze for up to 1 month.

Using a box grater or a food processor with a grating disc, coarsely grate the onion. Drain in a colander set in the sink or over a bowl. Peel and grate the carrot; set aside.

For the mango-habanero hot sauce, heat 1 tablespoon vegetable oil in a medium saucepan over medium-high heat. Add half the grated onion, the grated carrot, half the garlic, the mango, up to half the minced habanero (depending on how spicy you like it), and the vinegar. Cook until the vegetables are softened, about 5 minutes. Reduce the heat and cook, stirring occasionally, until the mixture is very soft and most of the liquid has evaporated, about 12 minutes. Let cool slightly, then blend in a blender until smooth, slowly drizzling in mango or orange juice until you have the desired consistency; you may not use all the juice. Season with salt. (This makes more than you'll need for these patties; cover and refrigerate the extra for up to 2 weeks.)

For the filling, heat the remaining 1 tablespoon vegetable oil in a large skillet over medium-high heat. Add the remaining onion and cook until softened, stirring often, about 2 minutes. Add the remaining garlic and ginger and cook another minute or so, stirring, until fragrant. Add the meat, as much of the remaining habanero as you want, the remaining 1 teaspoon curry powder, and the coriander, cumin, allspice, cloves, and thyme. Cook, breaking up with a wooden spoon, until well browned, 10 to 12 minutes. Reduce to medium-low heat. Add the rum, stirring occasionally until most of the liquid has evaporated, about 3 minutes. Season to taste with salt. Remove and let come to room temperature, then cover and refrigerate at least 20 minutes, or as long as 24 hours.

Line 2 baking sheets with parchment paper. On a lightly floured surface, use a lightly floured rolling pin to roll 1 square of chilled dough to about 10 x 10 inches, a generous ⅛ inch thick. Cut into 4 pieces about 5 x 5 inches. Carefully transfer to a prepared baking sheet, spacing well apart. Repeat with the second square of dough. Refrigerate until chilled, about 20 minutes.

Place oven racks in upper and center positions. Preheat the oven to 400°F.

Use a slotted spoon to heap ¼ cup filling on half of each dough square. Spread evenly, leaving a ½-inch border. Don't overfill, or it could be difficult to seal the pies. Brush the edges lightly with egg wash. Fold the empty side over the filling; use a fork to seal and crimp the edges and trim neatly to about ⅓ inch, if you wish. Brush the tops with egg wash. Space the pies well apart so they'll brown. Refrigerate until chilled, about 20 minutes.

Bake until golden brown, about 25 minutes; switch the sheets halfway through. Let cool on wire racks on the sheets at least 10 minutes. Serve warm or at room temperature with mango-habanero hot sauce.

Creamy Mushroom and Leek Demi-Lunes

The perfect "small bites" for a cocktail party, these vegetarian treats are elegant and easy to eat—on a plate or on a napkin. There's no juicy filling to ooze onto dress shoes at the first bite, and the flavors appeal to most palates. I call them "demi-lunes" because the filled pastry rounds are folded into half-moon shapes. Mine are a classic French combination of leek and mushroom, but once you've made them you'll see how easy it would be to change the filling endlessly.

MAKES ABOUT 36

Cream Cheese Crust (page 17)*

2 tablespoons unsalted butter, divided

3 leeks (white and pale green parts), halved lengthwise, thinly sliced cross-wise, rinsed and dried (about 6 cups)

Kosher salt and white pepper

8 ounces white button or cremini mushrooms, finely chopped (about 3 cups)

1 cup heavy cream

2 tablespoons minced fresh thyme leaves, plus more for sprinkling

Flour for rolling

2 egg yolks lightly beaten with 2 teaspoons water, for egg wash

* Other choices: Basic Pie Pastry (page 16), Extra-Rich Short Pastry (page 19), and Gluten-Free Pie Pastry (page 20).

Prepare the dough for the crust and shape it into 2 discs about 5 inches in diameter and ¾ inch thick. Wrap in plastic and refrigerate at least 1 hour (or up to 2 days), or freeze for up to 1 month.

Melt the butter in a large sauté pan or skillet over medium heat. When the foaming subsides, add the leeks and a big pinch each of salt and white pepper. Cook, stirring often, until softened but not yet beginning to color, about 6 minutes. Add the mushrooms and cook, stirring often, until the vegetables begin to color, about 8 minutes more. Season with another pinch of salt and pepper. Add the cream and thyme, scraping the bottom with a wooden spoon. Let come to a boil, then reduce to barely a simmer. Continue cooking, stirring occasionally, until the mixture thickens, 6 to 8 minutes. You should have a generous 2 cups. Let come to room temperature and then cover and refrigerate until chilled, at least 1 hour or up to overnight. (You can freeze the cooled filling, covered, for up to 1 month.)

On a lightly floured surface, use a lightly floured rolling pin to roll 1 dough disc into a large round a scant ⅛ inch thick. Use a 3½-inch cutter to cut about 18 dough circles, re-rolling the scraps if necessary. Transfer the circles to a parchment-lined baking sheet.

Repeat with the second dough disc, using a second lined baking sheet. Cover with plastic wrap and refrigerate about 20 minutes.

Place 2 teaspoons filling in the center of each chilled circle of dough; don't overfill, or they'll be difficult to seal. Moisten the edges with a little egg wash, using your finger, and fold into a half-moon shape; press the edges together to seal. Refrigerate on the baking sheets until chilled, at least 20 minutes. (These can be made up to 1 hour ahead and refrigerated, covered; or they can be frozen for up to 1 month, tightly covered in a single layer, and baked while still frozen.)

Meanwhile, place oven racks in upper and center positions. Preheat the oven to 400°F.

Just before baking, brush the exposed dough with egg wash and sprinkle with thyme. Bake until golden brown, 25 to 30 minutes; switch the sheets halfway through. Remove from the baking sheets and let cool on racks for 10 minutes. Serve warm.

NOTE

These demi-lunes can be baked as much as 8 hours ahead, kept at room temperature. Just before serving, reheat them for 10 to 12 minutes at 350°F.

"The Oggie" Steak and Stilton Pasty

"Oggie" is the traditional name for almost any pasty that contains rutabaga. "Pasty" is the pie itself—no matter the filling. It's probably a derivation of the word "pastry." Oggie or pasty, steak is the most sought-after filling. This is a workingman's pie, commonly eaten deep in the mines of central and northern England. It could be wrapped in cloth while fresh from the oven, then slowly unwrapped and eaten. Its shape made it easy for coal-stained hands to handle; once it got too small to leave wrapped in cloth, a miner could grasp the pointy pastry tip, biting it almost to the last coal-stained inch. Historians know this, because the mines of England are littered with countless pasty points. Well, not really. I made that last part up.

MAKES 8

Basic Pie Pastry (page 16)*

1¼ pounds skirt steak or beef chuck roast, cut into ½-inch or smaller dice (about 2 cups)

1 cup peeled, ⅓-inch-diced russet potato

¾ cup ¼-inch-diced onion

½ cup peeled, ⅓-inch-diced rutabaga or turnip

5 ounces English Stilton cheese, crumbled

3 tablespoons coarsely chopped fresh flat-leaf parsley

1 teaspoon kosher salt, plus more for sprinkling

½ teaspoon freshly cracked black pepper

Flour for rolling

¼ cup (½ stick) unsalted butter, cut into 8 chunks, divided

1 large egg yolk lightly beaten with 1 teaspoon water, for egg wash

* Other choices: Cream Cheese Crust (page 17), Extra-Rich Short Pastry (page 19), and Gluten-Free Pie Pastry (page 20).

Prepare the pastry dough and shape it into 2 discs about 5 inches in diameter and ¾ inch thick. Wrap in plastic and refrigerate at least 1 hour (or up to 2 days), or freeze for up to 1 month.

In a large bowl, mix together the meat, potato, onion, rutabaga or turnip, Stilton, and parsley. Season with 1 teaspoon salt and ½ teaspoon black pepper. Set aside.

On a lightly floured surface, use a lightly floured rolling pin to roll 1 chilled dough disc to a 12 or 13-inch round, a generous ⅛ inch thick. Cut out four 6-inch rounds, using a round cutter or a similar-size saucer and a knife; gather the scraps and re-roll as needed. Repeat with the second dough disc. Evenly space the rounds on 2 parchment-lined baking sheets.

Spoon a generous ½ cup meat filling onto each round, mounding it in the center and leaving a 1-inch border all around; don't overfill, or the pasties will be difficult to seal. Nestle a butter chunk into each mound. Brush the dough edges lightly with egg wash, carefully bring 2 sides up to meet at the top, and pinch the edges to seal. Decoratively crimp or scallop the edges as you like (see page 192). With the decorative edge facing up, brush on more egg wash and sprinkle with salt. Make 2 small slashes in the crust with the point of a sharp knife. Refrigerate on baking sheets until chilled, about 20 minutes.

While the pasties are chilling, place oven racks in upper and center positions. Preheat the oven to 400°F.

Bake the chilled pasties 10 minutes, then lower the oven temperature to 350°F and cook 20 more minutes. Switch the trays between racks and bake another 20 minutes, until golden brown (total baking time 50 minutes). Serve hot or at room temperature.

❧ WINE PAIRING

California Cabernet Sauvignon, preferably from the Napa Valley.

With a complex array of dark fruit, herb, earth, spice, and oak flavors, Cabernet is best when paired with robust yet simple foods. The wine's big tannins are mitigated by the fat in the beef. While pungent cheeses often aren't good with Cab, the Stilton in this pie is softened by the potatoes and rutabaga. Recommended producers: Corison, Rudius, Orin Swift.

Tilly's Pastelles

Tilly was my partner Ken's grandma. She made these pastelles her whole life—so many times and so well that there was no need for a recipe. But once she passed, Ken was afraid his grandma's particular version of this Sephardic classic would be gone as well. I know it could never be quite the same, but I've done my best to reproduce her recipe, based on his loving memories of his grandma and her meat pies.

MAKES 24

3 cups water, divided

1 cup plus 1 tablespoon vegetable oil, divided,

1½ teaspoons kosher salt, divided, plus more as needed

6 cups all-purpose flour, plus more as needed

1 large onion, finely diced (about 2 cups)

2 pounds ground beef

2 teaspoon dried oregano

1 teaspoon dried mint (optional)

1 teaspoon paprika

½ teaspoon ground cumin

¼ cup uncooked white rice

2 hard-cooked eggs, peeled and finely diced

½ cup minced fresh flat-leaf parsley

¼ cup sesame seeds, plus more for sprinkling

¼ teaspoon freshly cracked black pepper

2 egg yolks lightly beaten with 2 teaspoons water, for egg wash

In a large saucepan, bring 2½ cups water, 1 cup vegetable oil, and 1 teaspoon salt to a boil. Remove from heat and quickly stir in 6 cups flour, using a wooden spoon, until a soft dough forms. Scrape onto a lightly floured surface and knead, using more flour if necessary, until smooth, pliable, and not too sticky. Form into 24 balls about 2 inches in diameter (about 1½ ounces each) and 24 balls about 1½ inches in diameter (about ¾ ounce each). Place on parchment-lined baking sheets, cover with plastic wrap, and set aside at room temperature.

Heat the remaining 1 tablespoon oil in a large sauté pan over medium-high heat. Add the onion and cook until softened, stirring often, about 5 minutes. Add the ground meat, ½ teaspoon salt, oregano, mint, if using, cumin, and paprika. Cook, breaking up the meat with a wooden spoon, until well browned, 10 to 12 minutes. Reduce to very low heat and stir in the remaining ½ cup water and uncooked rice. Cover to cook the rice al dente, about 12 minutes. Uncover, remove from the heat, and stir in the hard-cooked egg, parsley, ¼ cup sesame seeds, and black pepper. Set aside to cool completely.

Place oven racks in the upper and center positions. Preheat the oven to 400°F.

Using your floured hands, shape the larger dough balls into cups 2½ to 3 inches wide and almost 1 inch deep. Return them to the prepared baking sheets as you work, about 1-inch apart. Divide the meat mixture among the cups, mounding it slightly (about ⅓ cup apiece).

On a lightly floured surface, use a lightly floured rolling pin or floured hands to roll or press the 1½-inch dough balls into 3-inch rounds. Cover each filled pastelle cup with a dough round, pinching the edges together in an upward motion to make a raised lip. If you wish, use a sharp, pointed knife to fringe the lip decoratively with short up and down motions. Brush the tops and sides with egg wash. Sprinkle the tops with salt and sesame seeds.

Bake until the pastelles are golden brown, 35 to 40 minutes; switch the sheets halfway through. Serve warm or at room temperature.

NOTE

The dried mint is optional, but it's what gives this version a particularly Turkish flair. This recipe is easily halved to make just a dozen pastelles.

BBQ Chicken Empanadas with Cilantro Chimichurri

It took me a while to warm up to those prebaked or rotisserie chickens you see at the market. I mean, how hard is it to roast a chicken? But a few years back I was at my local Latin market just as they were pulling a batch from the oven. They smelled so good and seemed so convenient that I bought one. Well, it made a convert out of me. Of course, you can roast a chicken yourself for this recipe, or you can use leftovers from a previous meal. But I'm giving you official permission to take a shortcut if you like, because you won't be sacrificing a thing.

MAKES 8

Cream Cheese Crust (page 17)*

1½ cups chopped fresh cilantro leaves, divided

¼ cup chopped fresh flat-leaf parsley

½ cup plus 2 tablespoons olive oil, divided

Juice of 2 limes

2 cloves garlic, minced

1 teaspoon kosher salt, divided

¾ teaspoon red pepper flakes, divided

1 small poblano chile (or Anaheim, if you prefer a milder taste)

1 medium red onion, halved and sliced (about 2 cups)

¾ pound shredded roast chicken meat, skin and bones removed

¾ cup sweet barbecue sauce of your choosing

3 ounces Monterey Jack cheese, shredded

Flour for rolling

1 egg yolk lightly beaten with 1 teaspoon water, for egg wash

* Other choices: Basic Pie Pastry (page 16), Extra-Rich Short Pastry (page 19), and Gluten-Free Pie Pastry (page 20).

Prepare the dough for the crust and shape it into 2 discs about 5 inches in diameter and ¾ inch thick. Wrap in plastic and refrigerate at least 1 hour (or up to 2 days), or freeze for up to 1 month.

To make the cilantro chimichurri, in the bowl of a food processor combine 1 cup cilantro, parsley, ½ cup olive oil, lime juice, garlic, and ½ teaspoon each of salt and red pepper. Pulse until finely chopped. Scrape into a small bowl and refrigerate at least 1 hour, or up to overnight.

Place oven racks in upper and center positions. Preheat the oven to 400°F.

On a piece of foil, drizzle the chile with 1 tablespoon olive oil; enclose in the foil, creating a tight packet. Roast on a baking pan on the center rack until softened, 20 to 30 minutes (depending on size). Turn off oven and remove them from the foil. When cool enough to handle, rub off the skin and remove the stem and seeds. Coarsely chop the flesh; set aside.

In a large sauté pan over medium heat, cook the onion slices with the remaining 1 tablespoon olive oil and a pinch of salt, stirring often, until well softened, about 8 minutes. Combine the cooked onions in a large bowl with the chicken, chopped chile, remaining ½ cup cilantro, barbecue sauce, cheese, remaining ½ teaspoon salt, and remaining ¼ teaspoon red pepper. Mix well, breaking up the meat with a wooden spoon. You should have a generous 4 cups of filling. Cover and refrigerate at least 20 minutes, or up to 24 hours.

Meanwhile, line 2 baking sheets with parchment paper. Divide 1 chilled dough disc into quarters, roll into balls, and flatten slightly with your hand. On a lightly floured surface, use a lightly floured rolling pin to roll into rounds about 6 inches in diameter and a generous ⅛ inch thick. Carefully transfer to a prepared baking sheet, spaced well apart. Repeat with the second dough disc. Refrigerate until chilled, about 20 minutes.

Keep the oven racks in upper and center positions. Reheat the oven to 400°F. Spread a scant ½ cup chilled filling on 1 side of each dough round, leaving a ½-inch border. Don't overfill, or it could be difficult to seal. Brush the edges lightly with egg wash. Fold the empty half over the filling into a half-moon so the edges meet; press together to seal and crimp or roll the edge decoratively. Trim the edges neatly to about ⅓ inch, if you wish. Brush the tops with egg wash. Refrigerate until chilled, about 20 minutes.

Bake until golden brown, about 25 minutes; switch the sheets halfway through. Let cool on wire racks on the baking sheets for at least 10 minutes. Serve warm or at room temperature with the cilantro chimichurri.

NOTE

Frying is also a common method of preparing empanadas. If you want to fry yours, skip the egg wash. Heat a scant inch of vegetable oil in a deep pan over medium-high heat until it registers 365°F. Fry 1 or 2 empanadas at a time, turning them once, until deeply golden, about 5 minutes. Return the oil to 365°F between batches.

Apple-Bacon-Onion Southern-Style Fried Pies

Go anywhere in the South and say "fried pie" and you'll get one of two reactions: scrunched eyebrows or raised eyebrows. The younger set is familiar with the fried pies kept under a heat lamp in the shadow of some golden arches; they'll likely scrunch their brows and say, "No, thank you." But some folks will raise their eyebrows and listen carefully, because they remember deliciously sweet fried pies made with fresh peaches in summer or dried apples in winter. My little pies take their cue from the apple variety. Loaded with bacon, onions, and lots of black pepper, they're decidedly savory. But man, are they sweet.

MAKES 10

Extra-Rich Short Pastry (page 19)*

1 teaspoon mild, sweet curry powder

4 extra-thick slices bacon

1 tablespoon unsalted butter

3 medium yellow onions, halved and thinly sliced

3 medium apples, peeled, cored, and thinly sliced

¼ cup water, plus more as needed

3 tablespoons apple cider vinegar

½ teaspoon freshly cracked black pepper

Kosher salt, as needed

Flour for rolling

Peanut or canola oil for frying

* Other choices: Basic Pie Pastry (page 16), Cream Cheese Crust (page 17), and Gluten-Free Pie Pastry (page 20).

Prepare the pastry recipe, adding the curry powder to the flour mixture. Divide the dough into 10 equal-size balls; flatten into ¾-inch-thick discs. Wrap in plastic and refrigerate at least 1 hour (or up to 2 days), or freeze for up to 1 month.

Place the bacon in a large, unheated cast-iron or other heavy-bottomed Dutch oven. Turn the heat to medium and cook, uncovered, until crisp on both sides, 8 to 10 minutes. Lift out and drain on paper towels, then crumble or chop coarsely into a large bowl.

Pour off all but about 2 tablespoons of the bacon fat. Return to medium heat and add the butter; increase to medium-high heat. Add the onions and cook until softened, stirring often, about 8 minutes. Add the apples and cook until softened, stirring often, about 6 more minutes.

Pour in ¼ cup water, cover, and reduce to very low heat. Cook, stirring occasionally, until the onions are caramelized and jammy and the apples are falling apart, about 50 minutes.

You may have to add a couple more tablespoons of water halfway through, depending on the moisture content of your onions.

Uncover and stir in the vinegar. Scrape the mixture into the bowl with the bacon and stir to combine. Adjust the seasoning with ½ teaspoon black pepper and salt to taste; you may not need much salt, depending on your bacon.

On a lightly floured surface, use a lightly floured rolling pin to roll each dough piece to about a 6-inch round. Place about ¼ cup filling on half of each circle, near the center; don't overfill, or they'll be difficult to seal. Moisten the dough edges with water, using your finger. Fold over into a half-moon so the edges meet; press together to seal. If you like, crimp decoratively with your fingers or a fork. As you work, move the pasties to a parchment-lined tray. Trim the sealed edges neatly to about ⅓ inch, if you wish. Refrigerate until chilled, about 20 minutes.

Meanwhile, fill a medium straight-sided pot with 4 inches of oil and heat to 365°F. Fry the pies in batches, rolling them around in the oil until golden, about 3 to 4 minutes. Use a slotted heatproof spoon to transfer the cooked pies to a paper towel–lined plate. Sprinkle immediately with salt. Serve hot (but not too hot).

Gruyère and Greens Turnovers

Many of us have fond childhood memories of eating flaky apple turnovers. When I was very young, I had a great-grandma who made them on special Sundays. One big bite sent crisp flakes of pastry all down the front of my "let's visit Grandma" clothes. I certainly thought that was funny, though my mom didn't. These days I prefer to keep my clothes neat and clean, and I like my pies savory. But that can't stop me from enjoying the mystifying crunch of those million flaky layers. Besides, wasn't it Grandma who said, "Eat your greens, Greg"?

MAKES 6

Kosher salt

2 (6-ounce) bags young greens (such as mustard, dandelion, spinach, kale)

1 tablespoon unsalted butter

1 medium shallot, minced

2 cloves garlic, minced

Pinch of cayenne pepper (or substitute cracked black pepper)

Flour for rolling

1 (14-ounce) package frozen all-butter puff pastry, thawed in the refrigerator*

1½ cups grated Gruyère cheese (this is the time to buy the good stuff)

1 large egg yolk lightly beaten with 1 teaspoon water, for egg wash

* 1½ sheets from a 17.3-ounce package of puff pastry can be cut into 5-inch squares and substituted for the 14-ounce package listed above.

Prepare an ice-water bath in a large bowl.

Bring a large saucepan of water to a boil; add a few big pinches of salt. Working with a couple handfuls at a time, quickly blanch the greens until well wilted (how long depends on the type of greens). Transfer to the ice bath as they finish to stop the cooking. Drain in a colander or salad spinner, then squeeze by fistfuls as dry as you can. Transfer to a cutting board and coarsely chop.

Melt the butter in a large skillet over medium-high heat. When the foam subsides, add the shallot and cook until softened, stirring often, about 1 minute. Add the garlic and cook a minute more. Turn off the heat and mix in the greens while the pan is still warm. Season with salt and a pinch of cayenne or black pepper. Set aside to cool.

On a lightly floured work surface, use a lightly floured rolling pin to roll the puff pastry to about a 10 x 15-inch rectangle, a scant ¼ inch thick. Trim cleanly, using a ruler and a pizza cutter or sharp knife, and then cut in half lengthwise to make 2 strips about 5 x 15 inches. Cut crosswise into thirds, giving you six 5-inch squares. Space evenly on 2 parchment-lined baking sheets (they'll brown better with plenty of space). If the dough seems quite soft, refrigerate for about 20 minutes.

Stir the Gruyère into the cooled greens and divide into 6 portions. Gently squeeze into dense, palm-size oval balls. Brush egg wash along the edges of the dough pieces, using your finger. Place a mound of greens in the center and fold the dough diagonally over the filling, creating a triangle; press the edges to seal. Brush with egg wash and sprinkle with a bit more salt (optional). Refrigerate until chilled, about 20 minutes.

Meanwhile, place oven racks in upper and center positions. Preheat the oven to 425°F. Bake the turnovers until puffed and golden brown, 16 to 18 minutes; switch the sheets halfway through. Serve warm or at room temperature.

Mushroom, Goat Cheese, and Mint Hand Pies

Savory little hand pies make a great on-the-go snack. This version is filled with goat cheese, mushrooms, and mint. Yes, mint. Make sure you choose spearmint, which is herbal in flavor and doesn't have the high menthol content that gives peppermint that cool mouth sensation.

My thanks to Russ Parsons of the Los Angeles Times *whose mushroom quesadilla inspired these pies.*

MAKES 8

Basic Pie Pastry (page 16)*

Flour for rolling

2 tablespoons unsalted butter

1 pound button mushrooms, sliced

½ teaspoon kosher salt, plus more for sprinkling

2 tablespoons minced shallot

2 tablespoons minced spearmint leaves

1 ounce crumbled fresh goat cheese, at room temperature

2 ounces low-moisture mozzarella cheese, cut into ½-inch dice

1 large egg yolk lightly beaten with 1 teaspoon water, for egg wash

* Other choices: Cream Cheese Crust (page 17), Extra-Rich Short Pastry (page 19), and Gluten-Free Pie Pastry (page 20).

Prepare the pastry dough and shape it into 2 squares about 5 x 5 inches and ¾ inch thick. Wrap in plastic and refrigerate at least 1 hour (or up to 2 days), or freeze for up to 1 month.

Melt the butter in a medium skillet over medium-high heat. Add the mushrooms and sprinkle with ½ teaspoon salt. Cook, stirring frequently, until the mushrooms have given up their moisture, about 5 minutes. Add the shallot and cook until softened, about 5 more minutes. Remove from the heat and stir in the mint and goat cheese until the mushroom mixture is well coated. Let come to room temperature.

On a lightly floured surface, use a lightly floured rolling pin to roll 1 dough square to about 10 or 11 inches square, a generous ⅛ inch thick. Use a paring knife to trim the edges neatly, then cut into four 5-inch squares. Place on a parchment-lined baking sheet about ½ inch apart. Repeat with the second square of dough. Divide the mozzarella among the squares, leaving a 1-inch border all around. Place 2 heaping tablespoons mushroom filling on top. Working a square at a time, fold all 4 corners over the filling so the points come near the center but don't touch (leave about ¼ inch between them). Press lightly to distribute the filling somewhat, being careful not to let any escape. Refrigerate until chilled, about 20 minutes.

While the pies are chilling, place an oven rack in the center position. Preheat the oven to 400°F.

Brush the tops and edges of the chilled pies with egg wash and sprinkle with salt. Bake until the pies are golden brown and filling is oozing out a little, about 25 minutes. Move to a wire rack to cool somewhat. Serve warm or at room temperature.

Rice and Egg Pirozhki with Green Onion and Dill

For some pies you just have to go to the source to find an authentic version. For these pirozhki I turned to Natasha Price, the talented cook and blogger behind 5 Star Foodie (www.fivestarfoodie .com)*. Originally from Kiev, Ukraine, she fondly remembers the foods of her childhood and has re-created many of them on her blog—which is where I found these little "pocket pies." They can be fried or baked with quite a variety of traditional fillings, both sweet and savory: apples, cherries, cheese, meat, mushrooms, and cabbage. In the spring, egg and green onion make a terrific filling for these delicious pastries.*

MAKES 8

⅔ cup whole milk, at room temperature, divided

1 teaspoon sugar

1 teaspoon dry yeast

1 egg, lightly beaten

2 tablespoons unsalted butter, melted, divided

Kosher salt

2 cups all-purpose flour, plus more for rolling

1 tablespoon water

4 green onions, white and light green parts finely chopped (about ¼ cup)

3 hard-cooked eggs, peeled and coarsely chopped

½ cup cooked white rice

1 teaspoon minced fresh dill

Freshly cracked black pepper

1 egg yolk lightly beaten with 1 teaspoon water, for egg wash

Warm ⅓ cup milk in a small bowl in the microwave. Stir in the sugar and yeast; let stand until foamy.

In a large bowl, combine the lightly beaten egg, 1 tablespoon melted butter, the remaining ⅓ cup milk, and a big of pinch of salt. Use a wooden spoon to stir in the yeast mixture, followed by the 2 cups flour in 4 or 5 additions until well incorporated. Cover with a clean kitchen towel and leave in a warm place for at least an hour, until it doubles in volume.

Place an oven rack in the center position. Preheat the oven to 375°F. Line a large baking sheet with parchment paper.

Meanwhile, add the remaining 1 tablespoon butter to a medium skillet over medium-high heat. Add the green onions and cook, stirring often, until softened and just beginning to color, about 6 minutes. Remove from the heat to cool slightly.

Push the hard-cooked eggs through a potato ricer into the skillet with the green onions, or finely dice and add. Stir in the rice and dill. Season with salt and pepper.

On a lightly floured surface, shape the dough into a log about 2 inches in diameter. Divide into 8 pieces and roll each one into a 6-inch round. Brush the edges with egg wash. Divide the filling among the rounds, heaping it in the center. Fold the dough over the filling and pinch the edges together to seal. Place seam side down on the prepared baking sheet, tucking the corners under to create an oval. Brush the exposed dough with egg wash.

Bake until puffed and golden, about 20 minutes. Serve warm or at room temperature.

NOTE

Frying is also a common method of preparing pirozhki. If you want to fry yours, skip the egg wash. Heat a scant inch of vegetable oil in a deep pan over medium-high heat until the oil registers 365°F. Fry 1 or 2 pirozhki at a time, turning once, until deeply golden, about 5 minutes. Return the oil to 365°F between batches.

Chickpea Samosas with Spicy Mint Sauce

This is India's version of street food perfection—a hand pie, of course. Every culture has one, but there's something about Indian samosas that has led the way in a worldwide surge in street-food culture.

MAKES 32

Spicy Mint Sauce

2 cups lightly packed fresh mint leaves

1 cup lightly packed cilantro sprigs

½ cup minced onion

1¼ cups water, divided

1 tablespoon fresh lime juice

1 teaspoon minced serrano chile

1 teaspoon sugar

Dough

1½ cups all-purpose flour, plus more for rolling

2 tablespoons semolina

1 teaspoon kosher salt

Pinch of ajwain seeds (optional, may be found in Indian markets or online)

2 tablespoons vegetable oil

¾ cup water

Filling

2 medium Yukon Gold potatoes, peeled and cut into 2-inch chunks

1 teaspoon kosher salt, plus more as needed

1 teaspoon Madras-style curry powder, or more to taste

2 tablespoons unsalted butter, melted

1 teaspoon vegetable oil

1 teaspoon cumin seeds

½ cup minced onion

1 small carrot, peeled and finely diced (about ½ cup)

1 teaspoon peeled and grated fresh ginger

1 teaspoon minced mild green chile

1 cup canned chickpeas, drained

½ cup frozen peas

2 teaspoons minced fresh chives

Freshly cracked black pepper, as needed

Peanut or canola oil as needed for frying

To make the mint sauce, combine the mint, cilantro, ½ cup minced onion, ½ cup water, lime juice, serrano chile, and sugar in a blender to form a rough purée. (The sauce may be made up to 2 days ahead and refrigerated, covered. Bring to room temperature to use.)

For the dough, in a medium bowl mix together 1½ cups all-purpose flour, semolina, 1 teaspoon salt, and ajwan seeds (if using). In another bowl mix together the oil and water.

(Don't try too hard—you know what they say about oil and water.) Stir the flour mixture into the oil mixture in 3 or 4 increments, mixing well between additions.

On a lightly floured surface, knead the dough, using more flour as needed until you have a smooth but fairly stiff dough. Press your thumb in to check—there should be almost no bounce-back in the indentation. Wrap in plastic and set aside to rest at room temperature at least 1 hour. (The dough may be made up to 2 days ahead and refrigerated, covered. Bring back to room temperature before continuing.)

For the filling, place the potato chunks and 1 teaspoon salt in a large saucepan. Add just enough water to cover by about 1 inch. Bring to a boil, then reduce to a simmer. Cover and cook until the potatoes fall apart when poked with a fork, about 20 minutes. Drain and return to the hot, dry pan. Turn the heat to low and cook, uncovered, shaking the pan often to evaporate as much water from the hot potatoes as you can, about 4 minutes. Let cool somewhat, then push through a ricer into a large bowl, or use a masher or fork. Stir in the curry powder and melted butter. Set aside.

Heat the vegetable oil in a large cast-iron or other heavy-bottomed skillet over medium-high heat. Add the cumin seeds. Once they begin to pop, add the onions and carrots. Cook until softened, stirring often, about 6 minutes. Stir in the ginger and mild green chile; cook about 1 minute. Set aside to cool somewhat, then add to the potatoes. Stir in the chickpeas, peas, and chives. Adjust the seasoning with salt and pepper as needed. Set aside. (The filling may be made up to 2 days ahead and refrigerated, covered. Bring to room temperature before continuing.)

To assemble the samosas, on a lightly floured surface form the dough into 16 balls, about 1¾ ounces each. Use a lightly floured rolling pin to roll into 6-inch rounds, a generous ⅛ inch thick; cut in half to create half-moons. Spoon a generous 2 tablespoons filling in the center of a half-moon; lightly moisten the dough edges with water, using your finger. Lift 1 corner and fold halfway over the filling at a 45° angle, aligning the straight edge down the center. Press lightly to seal the dough along the outer edge. Repeat with the other corner, creating a neat triangular packet. Pinch or crimp any openings shut. Repeat to form 32 small samosas.

Fill a medium straight-sided pot with 4 inches of oil and heat to 365°F. Fry the samosas in batches, rolling them around in the oil until golden, about 3 to 4 minutes per side. Use a slotted heatproof spoon to transfer them to a paper towel–lined plate as they finish cooking. Serve hot (but not too hot) with the mint sauce.

Egg Roll-Overs with Sweet Chili Sauce

Everyone loves egg rolls. But they don't have to be fried, and they don't have to be served with a sweet plum sauce. My puff pastry version of Chinese egg rolls comes with a sweet chili sauce that has plenty of heat. It's my favorite part of this recipe, so I don't mind if you double or triple the amount suggested here. The sauce will keep in the refrigerator, covered, for several days. Of course, you can buy similar hot sauces, but they lack zip. There's more to hot sauce than just heat.

MAKES 6

Sweet Chili Sauce

4 tablespoons water

2 tablespoons light brown sugar

1 small red Thai bird chile, thinly sliced crosswise (optional)

1 clove garlic, minced

1 tablespoon vegetable oil

1 tablespoon Asian fish sauce

Juice of 1 lime

3 tablespoons sambal oelek or similar Asian-style chili paste

2 tablespoons minced fresh mint leaves

Egg Roll-Overs

1 tablespoon vegetable oil

2 green onions (white, light green, and some dark green parts), thinly sliced (about ½ cup loosely packed)

1 clove garlic, minced

½ teaspoon mustard seeds

½ savoy cabbage, sliced slaw style (about 4 cups loosely packed)

2 carrots, peeled and coarsely shredded (about 1 cup moderately packed)

½ teaspoon kosher salt, plus more for sprinkling

½ cup chicken broth

1 teaspoon unseasoned rice vinegar

1 (14-ounce) package frozen all-butter puff pastry, thawed in the refrigerator*

1 egg yolk lightly beaten with 1 teaspoon water, for egg wash

2 teaspoons black sesame seeds

* Two sheets from a 17.3-ounce package of puff pastry can be stacked, folded, and rolled together as a substitute for the 14-ounce package listed above; you'll have pastry left over.

To make the sweet chili sauce, in a small saucepan heat the water, brown sugar, and chile slices (as many as you like), if using, over medium-high heat, swirling occasionally, until the liquid has thickened somewhat, about 3 minutes. Remove from heat; stir in the minced garlic, 1 tablespoon vegetable oil, fish sauce, lime juice, chili paste, and mint leaves. Set aside.

For the egg roll-overs, place an oven rack in the center position. Preheat the oven to 400°F.

Heat the oil in a medium sauté pan or skillet over medium-high heat. Add the green onion, garlic, and mustard seeds, stirring until fragrant, about 1 minute. Add the cabbage, carrot, and ½ teaspoon salt and sauté until softened, stirring occasionally, about 5 minutes. Stir in the broth and continue cooking, stirring occasionally, until the pan is nearly dry, about 5 minutes. Stir in the rice vinegar; remove and let come to room temperature. (The filling can be made up to 8 hours ahead and refrigerated, covered.)

On a lightly floured surface, use a lightly floured rolling pin to roll the puff pastry to a 10 x 15-inch rectangle, a scant ¼ inch thick. Using a paring knife and a straightedge, trim the edges neatly. Cut into six 5-inch squares.

Spoon a generous ¼ cup of the vegetable mixture across the lower third of each square, leaving a ½-inch border at the edges. Fold in the sides, covering the filling by about ½ inch. Then roll the bottom edge up and over the filling, jelly-roll fashion, creating a 4-inch tube about 2½ inches in diameter. Place seam-side down on a parchment-lined baking sheet. Brush with egg wash and sprinkle with sesame seeds.

Bake until puffed and golden brown, about 20 minutes. Serve warm with sweet chili sauce.

Duck Confit Taquito Pies with Goat Cheese Dipping Sauce

I stole this recipe for pulled duck confit with mole spices from my brother Grant. It's not really a mole, but that's part of its genius. It's so good I just had to find a way to squeeze it into a pie. I chose to roll it taquito-style into a chili-cumin wrapper of all-butter Basic Pie Pastry and then deep fry it. Why not, right? I love the way the bits of exposed duck turn crisp and crackly in the fryer. But I can also imagine this filling baked into a traditional hand pie with any crust you like. Or serve it as a true taquito or taco with handmade corn tortillas. Grant likes to fold it into cornmeal empanada dough. Of course, you could just eat it straight from the skillet and save yourself all these decisions.

MAKES 12

For the Dipping Sauce

8 ounces fresh goat cheese (such as Montrachet), at room temperature

⅔ cup Greek-style yogurt

2 tablespoons fresh lime juice

2 tablespoons minced fresh cilantro (optional)

Kosher salt and freshly cracked black pepper

For the Taquitos

Basic Pie Pastry (page 16)*

2 teaspoons chili powder

¼ teaspoon ground cumin

Flour for rolling

2 prepared duck confit legs with skin, bones, and thigh meat attached (about 1½ pounds)

⅓ cup ¼-inch-diced red onion

2 teaspoons Dutch-process cocoa powder

½ teaspoon ground cinnamon

Pinch of ground cloves

1 canned chipotle chile in adobo, finely chopped

2 fresh apricots, coarsely chopped

½ cup water

Peanut or canola oil, as needed for frying

* Other choices: Cream Cheese Crust (page 17), Extra-Rich Short Pastry (page 19), and Gluten-Free Pie Pastry (page 20).

To make the dipping sauce, blend the goat cheese, yogurt, and lime juice in a mini food processor or blender until smooth. Transfer to a small bowl and stir in the cilantro, if using. Season to taste with a pinch each of salt and pepper. Cover and refrigerate at least 1 hour, or up to 24 hours.

For the taquitos, prepare the pastry, adding the chili powder and cumin to the flour mixture. Shape the dough into 2 rectangles about 5 x 6 inches and ¾ inch thick. Wrap in plastic and refrigerate at least 1 hour (or up to 2 days), or freeze for up to 1 month.

Working on a lightly floured piece of parchment paper sized to fit rimless baking sheets, use a lightly floured rolling pin to roll 1 piece of chilled dough into a rectangle at least 8 x 12 inches, a scant ⅛ inch thick. Move the dough on the parchment to the baking sheet. Use a paring knife to trim neatly to 8 x 12 inches and then cut into six 4-inch squares. Repeat with the second piece of dough and a second baking sheet. Cover lightly with plastic wrap and refrigerate at least 20 minutes.

For the filling, season the prepared duck confit legs with salt and pepper. Heat a large cast-iron or heavy-bottomed nonstick skillet over medium-low heat. Place the duck legs, skin-side down, in the dry, hot skillet. Cover and cook, turning occasionally, until the skin is well browned and crisp and the duck is heated through, about 20 minutes. Transfer to a paper towel–lined plate to cool somewhat. Pour off all but about 1 teaspoon of fat from the skillet (reserve the extra for another use).

Return the skillet to the stove and raise the heat to medium. Add the onion, cocoa powder, cinnamon, and cloves. Cook, stirring almost constantly, until the onions are caramelized, about 10 minutes. Add the chipotle and apricot and cook a minute more. Add the water, allow it to sizzle a moment, and scrape the bottom with a wooden spoon to loosen the browned bits. Continue cooking, scraping occasionally, until you have a thick, chunky sauce, about 6 more minutes. Pour into a medium bowl.

Once the duck is cool enough, remove the skin and set it aside. Remove the meat from the bones, shred, and add to the bowl with the onion sauce. Stir to combine, adding a pinch of salt if needed.

Place the reserved duck skin in a clean, dry cast-iron or heavy-bottomed nonstick skillet over medium heat. Cook until very crisp, watching carefully and turning as needed, about

5 minutes. Chop coarsely and add to the sauced meat, stirring to combine. Save the duck fat from the skillet for another use.

To assemble, use your finger to moisten the back edge of a pastry square with water. Spread a scant ¼ cup duck filling across the front of the square, leaving a ½-inch border only in front. Roll the dough back over the filling to form a tube, a generous 1 inch in diameter. Press the back edge to seal. Repeat with the other squares.

Line a large plate with a double layer of paper towels. Fill a medium straight-sided pot with 4 inches of peanut or canola oil and heat to 365°F. Fry the taquito pies in batches, occasionally rolling them in the oil with a heatproof utensil, until lightly golden, about 3 to 4 minutes. Don't let the exposed meat get too fried—crisp duck is delicious, but burnt is boring. Use a slotted spoon to transfer them to the lined plate. Sprinkle with salt. Serve hot (but not too hot) with the dipping sauce.

Aussie "Dog's Eye" Lamb Pie with Fig Ketchup

Meat pies are iconic in Australia. If this recipe treads on some Aussie traditions, forgive me and look to my intentions. I'm fully aware that there are standards for this pie: the filling should be quite sloppy, without much flour for thickening; there shouldn't be any visible vegetables, except maybe finely chopped onion; and there should be just enough pepper to give your tongue a tingle. And for reasons I can't quite understand, the pie must always have a shortcrust bottom and a puff pastry top. Here's the kicker: "dog's eye pies" are always served with ketchup (or rather, tomato sauce). My version comes with a tongue-tingling fig ketchup, which may send arms flailing toward heaven in pie shops from Perth to Brisbane.

MAKES 12

Extra-Rich Short Pastry (page 19)*

1 pound fresh figs, trimmed and quartered

½ pound tomatoes, diced (use a "paste" variety such as Roma)

1 teaspoon coriander seeds

1 teaspoon cumin seeds

½ cup packed dark brown sugar

1 cup malt vinegar, plus more to taste

3 tablespoons pomegranate molasses (or substitute honey)

1 teaspoon Asian-style chili paste

¼ teaspoon cayenne pepper, or to taste

1 cinnamon stick

1 bay leaf

6 slices bacon

1 medium onion, finely diced

Kosher salt

1 pound ground lamb

1 tablespoon Worcestershire sauce

¼ teaspoon red pepper flakes

1 tablespoon all-purpose flour, plus more for rolling

1 cup beef broth

1 tablespoon minced fresh flat-leaf parsley

Cooking spray

1 (14-ounce) package frozen all-butter puff pastry, thawed in the refrigerator*

1 egg yolk lightly beaten with 1 teaspoon water, for egg wash

Poppy seeds or sesame seeds, as needed

* Two sheets from a 17.3-ounce package of puff pastry can be stacked, folded, and rolled together as a substitute for the 14-ounce package listed above; you'll have pastry left over.

Prepare the pastry dough and shape it into 2 discs about 5 inches in diameter and ¾ inch thick. Wrap in plastic and refrigerate at least 1 hour (or up to 2 days), or freeze for up to 1 month.

To make the fig ketchup, place oven racks in upper and center positions and preheat the oven to 400°F. Line 2 rimmed baking sheets with parchment paper and spread the figs on one of the sheets, the tomatoes on the other. With the tomatoes on the top rack and the figs in the center, roast until they begin to color, about 15 minutes for the figs and 20 minutes for the tomatoes. As they finish roasting move the sheets to a wire rack, then turn off the oven.

In a medium saucepan, toast the coriander and cumin seeds over medium heat until fragrant, about 1 minute. Add the roasted figs and tomatoes, scraping up as much of the juice and crusty parts as possible, followed by the brown sugar, vinegar, pomegranate molasses, chili paste, cayenne pepper, cinnamon stick, and bay leaf. Raise the heat to high and let the mixture come to a boil, then reduce to very low and simmer, stirring often, until thick and jamlike, about 30 minutes. Let cool.

Discard the cinnamon stick and bay leaf. In a blender or food processor, thoroughly purée the mixture, adding a splash of vinegar to achieve the proper consistency, if necessary. Taste and adjust the acidity with more vinegar, if needed. Cover and chill for several hours. (This makes more than you need for these pies, but it will keep in the refrigerator for up to 2 weeks. It's very nice with most grilled meats, even burgers.)

To make the filling, place the bacon slices in a large, unheated cast-iron or other heavy-bottomed Dutch oven. Turn the heat to medium and cook until crisp, turning often, about 8 minutes. Transfer to a paper towel–lined plate. Coarsely chop or crumble and set aside.

Pour off all but about 2 tablespoons of the bacon fat. Raise the heat to medium-high and add the onion and a pinch of salt to the pot. Cook until softened somewhat, stirring often, about 6 minutes. Add the ground lamb, breaking it up with a wooden spoon, and cook until crumbly and well browned, 10 to 12 minutes. Reduce the heat to low and stir in the Worcestershire and red pepper. Sprinkle 1 tablespoon flour over the mixture, stir to incorporate, and cook about 1 minute. Slowly stir in the broth and simmer about 10 minutes. Taste and adjust the seasoning, if needed. Stir in the parsley. Set aside to cool.

❧ WINE PAIRING

Australian Shiraz, preferably from Barossa or McLaren Vale.

This wine is known for its bold and deep fruit flavors of berries with black pepper, spice, and mint. With its full body and mouth-filling texture, Australian Shiraz makes a nice match for this hearty lamb pie. The fruit and spice flavor combination in the ketchup is also well supported by the wine. Recommended producers: Two Hands, Yalumba, d'Arenberg.

To make the pie shells, use cooking spray to lightly coat the cups of a 12-portion standard-size muffin tin.

On a lightly floured surface, use a lightly floured rolling pin to roll 1 chilled dough disc to a 13-inch round, a generous ⅛ inch thick. Cut pastry circles large enough to fill the muffin cups, about 4 to 5 inches across depending on the muffin tin. Re-roll the scraps if necessary. Repeat with the second dough disc.

Gently line the muffin cups with the pastry rounds, trimming the overhang to about ½ inch. Prick the bottoms with a fork. Refrigerate until chilled, about 20 minutes.

Keep the oven racks in upper and center positions. Reheat the oven to 400°F

Place large parchment-paper baking cups in the dough-lined muffin compartments. Fill with pie weights, copper pennies, beans, or rice and bake until set but not fully cooked, about 14 minutes. Remove the liners and weights. Set the muffin tin on a rack to cool somewhat. Raise the oven temperature to 425°F.

To assemble the pies, divide the lamb mixture among the pastry shells, filling to the top. You may have extra filling, depending on your muffin tin.

On a lightly floured surface, use a lightly floured rolling pin to roll the puff pastry to a 10 x 15-inch rectangle, a scant ¼ inch thick. Cut 12 circles slightly larger than the muffin compartments; save the trimmings for another use.

Brush the pie edges with egg wash. Top each pie with a puff-pastry circle, tucking in the edges. Brush with more egg wash and sprinkle with poppy or sesame seeds. Bake until puffed and golden, about 20 minutes. Let cool on a wire rack at least 15 minutes before removing from the tin. Serve warm or at room temperature, topped with fig ketchup.

CONVERSIONS

MEASURE	EQUIVALENT	METRIC
1 teaspoon	--	5.0 milliliters
1 tablespoon	3 teaspoons	14.8 milliliters
1 cup	16 tablespoons	236.8 milliliters
1 pint	2 cups	473.6 milliliters
1 quart	4 cups	947.2 milliliters
1 liter	4 cups + 3½ tablespoons	1000 milliliters
1 ounce (dry)	2 tablespoons	28.35 grams
1 pound	16 ounces	453.49 grams
2.21 pounds	35.3 ounces	1 kilogram
375°F/425°F/500°F	--	190°C/218°C/260°C

RECIPE INDEX

ABOUT THE AUTHORS

GREG HENRY began to write the food blog *Sippity Sup—Serious Fun Food* as a break from a career as an entertainment industry photographer, and was surprised by its hold on him. He now writes a Friday column on entertaining for "The Back Burner" at Key Ingredient (www.keyingredient.com) and is active in the food blogging community. He's led cooking demonstrations in Panama and Costa Rica and has journeyed as far afield as Norway to promote culinary travel. He's been featured in *Food & Wine* magazine, the *Los Angeles Times*, *More* magazine, the *Today* show online, the *Huffington Post*, and *Saveur* magazine's "Best of the Web." Greg also cohosts "The Table Set" (downloadable on iTunes or at Homefries.com), named by *LA Weekly* as one of five favorite podcasts for food lovers. He and Grant are brothers, and this is their first book.

GRANT HENRY is a graduate of the French Culinary Institute (now the International Culinary Center) in New York City. He is recognized as a Certified Specialist of Wine by the Society of Wine Educators. Currently living in his hometown of St. Petersburg, Florida, Grant is a sales rep for a small wine distributor specializing in boutique wineries from around the world. When not selling wine, making delicious dinners for his friends and family, or entertaining his son, Grant puts the "Sip" in *Sippity Sup*. His three favorite wine words are *dirt*, *acid*, and *gravel*.

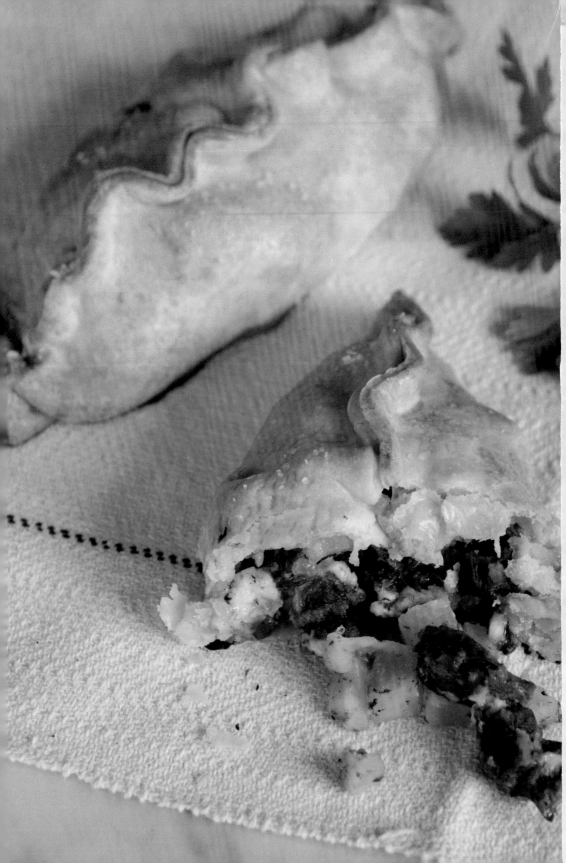